A Pocket Guide
to Holiday
Brittany

*Patricia McAuley
and Colette Martin*

HARRAP
London

ACKNOWLEDGEMENTS

The authors would like to thank the French Government Tourist Office and the Brittany Chamber of Commerce in London and the Regional and Departmental Offices and Loisirs Accueil in France who have supplied a wealth of information.

First published in Great Britain 1991
by Harrap Books Ltd
Chelsea House, 26 Market Square, Bromley, Kent BR1 1NA

© Colette Martin and Patricia McAuley 1991

Maps by Carole Vincer

ISBN 0 245-60259-3

Printed and bound in Great Britain by Richard Clay Ltd,
Bungay, Suffolk

CONTENTS

INTRODUCTION TO BRITTANY

Jutting out into the sea which dominates its landscape, customs, way of life and superstitions, Brittany still remains one of the most popular tourist regions of France. Year after year its unique charm attracts holidaymakers from all over France, the rest of Europe and further afield.

Although part of France, Brittany has its own distinctive character – even its own language which is still spoken in the more remote areas. Populated by the Celts in the fifth century, the Bretons, like the Irish, the Welsh and the Scots, have retained the Celtic sense of mystery, the love of legend, music and dance and loyalty to old traditions. Part of everyday life, these are highlighted in the numerous Breton celebrations. During the summer months local *fêtes* (festivals) abound. Regional costumes and beautiful headdresses are much in evidence and the dancers move to the resounding and sometimes eerie tones of the Breton pipes. Since religion plays an important part in Brittany's heritage there are fine churches, cathedrals and abbeys to be found everywhere and superbly carved calvaries with large groups of sculptured figures.

The savage beauty of the jagged coast contrasts strongly with the miles of safe, sandy beaches and rocky coves. Large and small resorts, many with harbours and marinas, are dotted along over seven hundred miles of coastline – ideal for family holidays and water sports enthusiasts. Despite its popularity, there are so many beaches that they never become overcrowded.

Uncluttered roads pass through ancient towns and villages, many huddling beneath massive fortified castles – a reminder of their feudal past – and cut across a varied landscape of heathered hillsides, lush green fields, deep forests, rivers and

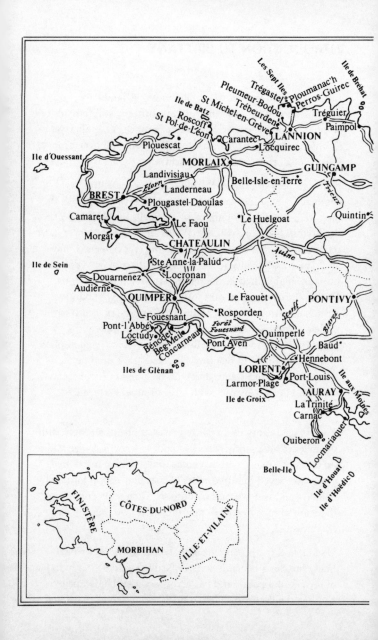

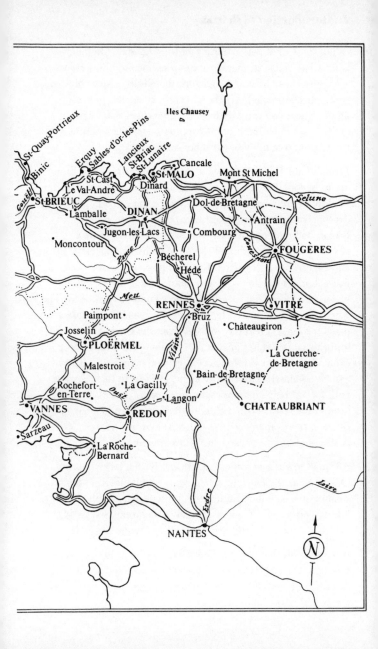

canals, making it perfect for a motoring holiday. On lonely windswept moors strange formations of huge standing stones and cairns bear witness to religions thousands of years old. In complete contrast market days in country towns are lively affairs where you can buy fresh local produce, cider and cheeses, antiques, hand-painted pottery, etc. They normally finish around midday so get there early.

Probably the largest number of artists and craftsmen in France are to be found living and working in Brittany. Many of their workshops are open to the public where you can see fine stone-carving, cabinet-making, lacework, embroidery, weaving and Breton doll-making. Brittany is now considered France's foremost region for golf and there are many fine courses. Riders and cyclists are well catered for, with bridlepaths and cycle-tracks both along the coast and inland, and walkers will find waymarked footpaths clearly numbered and colour-coded. The whole region is traversed by a network of waterways making it possible to take a leisurely journey from the north coast to the south by canal cruiser or east to west along the Nantes-Brest canal. There is good fishing on rivers and lakes and a permit can be obtained locally. Birdwatchers will be in their element with several bird sanctuaries on the many offshore islands and around the coast. With a climate that is mild and invigorating Brittany boasts many centres of hydrotherapy and thalassotherapy (sea-water health treatments).

All small towns and sometimes villages have a local Tourist Office (*Syndicat d'Initiative*) where you will find information on local events, activities, sightseeing, museums, accommodation, fishing permits etc. They can usually also supply maps and itineraries and generally help with all your enquiries.

Brittany is divided into the four *départements* of Côtes-du-Nord, Finistère, Ille-et-Vilaine and Morbihan, each of which is described individually in the following pages along with many towns and resorts of interest.

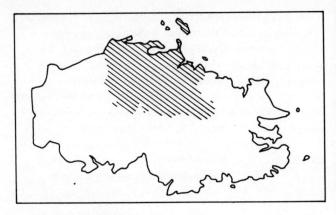

COTES-DU-NORD

Situated on the channel coast it is also known as the Côtes
d'Armor (Armor meaning 'country by the sea'). There are
no major cities in this rural area where remote country roads
traverse the typically Breton landscape of lush green
vegetation interspersed with lonely moorlands of heather
and broom. From the gorse-lined coastal paths there are
spectacular views of the distinctive coastline – jagged rocks,
windswept headlands, lagoons, inlets and islets. From the
Côte de Granit Rose in the west to the Côte d'Eméraude in
the east, dozens of small family resorts, yacht harbours and
picturesque ports shelter beneath pink granite cliffs bordered
by an emerald green sea. You can find beautiful beaches of
fine golden sand all along the coast, perhaps the best being
at Le Val-André and Perros-Guirec. Both these resorts offer
a wealth of facilities for the holiday-maker and in particular
the water sports enthusiast. Nearby at Ploumanac'h and
Trégastel the gradual erosion of the rocks has resulted in a
weird and wonderful display of animal and man-like
sculptures appropriately named 'the Elephant', 'the
Tortoise', 'the Witch' and 'Napoleon's Hat', to mention but

a few. Just offshore is Les Sept Isles (The Seven Islands) bird
sanctuary where a vast array of seabirds, penguins and
puffins nest safely. During the summer months there are
regular excursions to these islands from Perros-Guirec. Of
the many rocky promontories with panoramic views out to
sea, the most dramatic are Cap Fréhel, from whose 70-metre
high red-granite cliffs the Channel Islands can be seen on a
clear day, and Pointe de l'Arcouest. From the latter take a
ten-minute boat trip to the Ile de Bréhat. Its tiny creeks and
bays, lobster pots, flower-filled gardens and landscape of
purple heathland, gorse and mimosa make it a painter's
paradise.

Inland, Guingamp, Lamballe and St-Brieuc are attractive
and important agricultural centres. The ancient towns of
Lannion and Tréguier are interesting to visit as are the
fortified castles of Tonquédec and La Latte (Fréhel) and the
15th-century chapels of Loc Envel and Loc Maria in a
delightful wooded setting near Belle-Isle-en-Terre. The most
frequented tourist centre is undoubtably Dinan, one of the
best-preserved medieval towns in Britanny, and a setting-off
point for boat trips along the beautiful, winding river Rance.
Other famous beauty spots include the dramatic Gorges du
Daoulas and the nearby Lac de Guerlédan. It's an enormous
stretch of water popular with sailors and fishermen,
encircled by marked paths for walking and trekking.

Golfers are well catered for with several excellent nine- and
eighteen-hole courses and the scientifically minded will enjoy
seeing the Space Telecommunications Centre at Pleumeur-
Bodou.

TOWNS AND RESORTS OF INTEREST (Côtes-du-Nord)

Belle-Isle-en-Terre (60 km west of St-Brieuc)

Set in a particularly beautiful part of the countryside where the river Léguer meets the river Guic, Belle-Isle-en-Terre is an ideal centre for touring. Every July a Breton wrestling championship is held here, wrestling being an ancient Breton sport.

Binic (10 km north-west of St-Brieuc)
A delightful small resort on the west side of the Bay of St-Brieuc. Colourful cafes and restaurants line the waterfront. Formerly a cod-fishing port it is now mainly used by pleasure craft.

Dinan (36 km east of St-Brieuc)
Standing high above the beautiful river Rance, the fortified medieval town of Dinan probably attracts more visitors than any other town in Brittany. A curious 15th-century Clock Tower stands in the old town and nearby 15th- and 16th-century timbered houses, craft and antique shops line the winding, cobbled streets that lead down to the little yacht harbour. From the terraces of the *Jardin Anglais* (English Garden) there is a superb view of the Rance. From the gardens, descend by the twisting path that leads to quaint riverside houses and the old Gothic bridge. Pleasant walks too along the shady, tree-lined promenades that skirt the enormous granite ramparts. Inside the massive 14th-century castle is the very interesting museum of local history. River-boat excursions leave from Dinan for St-Malo and Dinard and follow the winding river Rance through pretty countryside.

Erquy (25 km north-east of St-Brieuc)
An attractive small fishing-port specializing in scallops. There are many fine beaches nearby.

Jugon-les-Lacs (20 km south-west of Dinan)
A *station verte* (pleasant inland holiday resort) with lovely old houses near several large lakes which are excellent for swimming, sailing and fishing.

Guingamp (31 km west of St-Brieuc)
An important agricultural centre, Guingamp attracts large
crowds in the first week of July when the annual *pardon* is
celebrated with fireworks and a candlelight procession, and
in August to its *Fête des Danses Bretonnes*. In the town square
a Renaissance fountain is surrounded by interesting old
granite houses. The nearby Basilica of Notre-Dame-de-Bon-
Secours is half Gothic, half Renaissance (the south side
collapsed and was rebuilt in the 16th century) and has very
fine carved doorways.

Lamballe (21 km south-east of St-Brieuc)
The Gothic Cathedral of Notre-Dame-de-Grande-Puissance
overlooks this quiet market town. Some fine old houses can
be found in the Place du Martrai including the 16th-century
Maison du Bourreau (Executioner's House) which now houses
the *Syndicat d'Initiative* and two museums. To the west of the
town centre, the Harras stud with over 200 stallions will be
of interest to horse-lovers.

Lancieux (20 km north-west of Dinan)
A simple resort with a wide sandy beach on the Côte
d'Eméraude.

Lannion (32 km north-west of Guingamp)
This old country town and port dating back to the 6th
century is built on the side of a hill on the banks of the river
Léguer. On the right bank of the river is old Lannion and
one of its main attractions, the 12th-century church of
Brélévenez, reached by a flight of 142 steps. From the
terraces there is a superb view of the surrounding
countryside. Lannion makes a good base for visiting the
resorts of the Côte de Granit Rose. Three kilometres north is
an important centre for electronics and telecommunications.

Moncontour (23 km south of St-Brieuc)
A flower-filled medieval town built on a promontory where
two river valleys meet. It can boast some fine old granite

houses and six magnificent stained-glass windows in the church of St-Mathurin. The nearby castle of La Touche-Trébry is worth a visit.

Paimpol (45 km north-west of St-Brieuc)
The thriving cod industry of the 19th century has long gone and the port of Paimpol is now used mainly by pleasure craft. The cultivation of oysters continues to thrive here and reminders of the town's long associations with the sea can be found in the Maritime Museum. Golf course: 10 km away. Boats for the delightful island of Bréhat leave from Arcouest Point a few miles to the north.

Perros-Guirec (75 km north-west of St-Brieuc)
A large sophisticated resort with a fishing-port and marina, a casino, elegant houses and hotels and two superb beaches – the Plage Trestraou and the Plage Trestrignel. It gets its name from the Breton word '*Pennroz*', meaning 'top of the hill', and indeed the town centre stands high on a hillside overlooking the port and the beaches. Above the sailing school at the west end of the town is the start of the *Sentier des Douaniers* (Path of the Customs Officers) which runs all the way to the resort of Ploumanac'h. From this delightful coastal path there are superb views of Les Sept Isles (Seven Islands) and below the pink granite cliffs a coastline of creeks and inlets and weirdly shaped rock sculptures. Motor launches leave from Trestraou beach for Les Sept Isles bird sanctuary. Landing is only allowed at the *Ile aux Moines* (Monks Island) where you can visit the lighthouse and fort.

Pleumeur-Bodou (10 km north-west of Lannion)
The giant white dome and antennae of the Space Telecommunications Centre dominate the surrounding lonely heathland. Guided tours of this world-famous Centre are available throughout the year. There is an 18-hole golf course nearby.

Ploumanac'h (7 km west of Perros-Guirec)

A pleasant resort with a small harbour and beautiful
sheltered beach, the Plage St-Guirec. At one end of the
beach stands a granite statue of St Guirec who landed here
in the 6th century. The statue was originally made of wood
but suffered badly from the old tradition whereby young
girls wanting husbands stuck pins in its nose. Crowds flock to
this part of the Pink Granite Coast to see the weirdly shaped
rock formations, many resembling animals, mentioned on
page three. Take the path between Ploumanac'h and
Perros-Guirec called the *Sentier des Douaniers* (Path of the
Customs Officers) for fabulous views over the rocks.
Wonderful views too from the lantern platform of the
lighthouse.

Quintin (20 km south-west of St-Brieuc)
The old granite houses of this charming small town rise in
terraces overlooking the river Gouët. Some traces of the
original ramparts remain; and what is said to be a fragment
of the Virgin Mary's belt brought to France by a Crusader
in the 13th century is one of the interesting relics in the
Basilica.

Sables-d'Or-les-Pins (28 km north-east of St-Brieuc)
As its name suggests, this small family resort has a beach of
golden sand backed by pine trees. 9-hole golf course.

St-Brieuc (31 km east of Guingamp)
This busy city, the commercial and administrative centre of
the department, is built in a commanding position on a
plateau between two waterways, their valleys spanned by
several bold viaducts. Though not as picturesque as some
other Breton towns, it has a lively town centre, wide
promenades, a busy port and is well known for its colourful
markets and fairs. Three different points on the headland
afford extensive views of the surrounding countryside,

namely: Rond-Point Huguin, Tertre Aubé and Tertre Notre-Dame.

St-Cast-le-Guildo (32 km north-west of Dinan)
A busy, small resort at the end of a peninsula on the Emerald Coast. A long beach of fine sand lies between Pointe St-Cast to the west and Pointe La Garde to the east, with superb views from both. There is a 9-hole golf course.

St-Michel-en-Grève (18 km south-west of Lannion)
This small resort lies in a particularly attractive part of the Armorican corniche. The *Lieue de Grève* (league of beach), a magnificent sweep of beach backed by pinetrees, stretches for 5 kilometres to the south and west.

St-Quay-Portrieux (21 km north-west of St-Brieuc)
This popular seaside resort boasts four good beaches, a casino and a yacht harbour. There are wonderful views of the bay of St-Brieuc from the gorse-lined coast road that starts at Portrieux and goes on for two miles along this scenic stretch of coastline. There is an 18-hole golf course nearby.

Trébeurden (9 km north-west of Lannion)
The main two beaches of this family resort lie on either side of the rocky peninsula Le Castel. From this vantage point the north coast of Finistère is visible on a clear day.

Trégastel-Plage (13 km north of Lannion)
As at Ploumanac'h a multitude of pink grey rocks eroded into weird and wonderful shapes are to be found here, particularly on the stretch of beach known as the *Grève Blanche* (white shore). In the little town of Trégastel there is a fine 12th-century church and beyond the village an interesting Breton calvary stands on a high mound facing the sea.

Tréguier (60 km north-west of St-Brieuc)
A terraced city on the side of a hill whose quiet streets slope down to a wide estuary. Standing at the junction of the

rivers Guindy and Jaudy, this capital of the Trégor region, particularly Breton in character, is probably best known as the birthplace of St Yves, the patron saint of lawyers and a friend of the poor. The annual *pardon* on 19 May is a colourful event with members of the legal profession from all over France joining in the procession. St Yves is buried in the magnificent Gothic Cathedral of St-Tugdual. The medieval glass in its sixty-eight windows was destroyed during the Revolution but has been skilfully replaced with modern stained-glass portraying Biblical themes. Visit also the cloisters and the treasure room. The Trégor coastline is a delightful area to explore, with tiny resorts nestling in sheltered inlets.

Le Val-André (29 km north-east of St-Brieuc)
A really lively resort with all the facilities the visitor could wish for. Its curving beach nearly 3 kilometres long is of the finest sand and the promenade runs all the way to the adjoining village of Pléneuf, with which it has close links. Walkers will make for the clifftop paths particularly round the Pointe de Pléneuf and along the Promenade de la Guette, from where there are extensive views of the wild and dramatic coastline of the Bay of St-Brieuc.

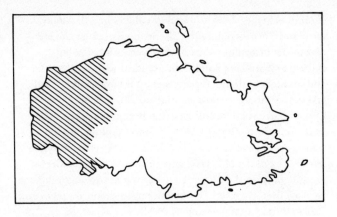

FINISTERE

Located at the western tip of Brittany, Finistère has a jagged coastline of mighty headlands and rocky promontories that jut out into the sea, small creeks, deep estuaries and wide sandy bays. Lying offshore are several islands – Batz, Molène, Sein and the Glénans – ranging from the wild and desolate to those which are quite well populated. Their attractions include bird sanctuaries, lighthouses, deserted strands, crystaline waters for swimming and diving, a large sailing school, inns, restaurants and ancient ruins. The whole coast is punctuated with small resorts, most with harbours and sailing schools (well over thirty) and conditions are good for sea cruising and fishing, windsurfing and all the water sports. Resorts such as Bénodet, Beg-Meil and Concarneau, long popular with the British as well as the French, remain comparatively unspoilt and offer fine sandy beaches and plenty of sports activities. There are coastal paths everywhere for walking and magnificent scenery whether your taste is for sheer cliff faces constantly sprayed by giant waves or for picture-book views of sandy bays with multi-coloured sails bobbing on a blue sea.

Inland, old stone-built towns and villages huddle among farmlands, heathered moors, in the forests, under the hills and in the beautiful valley of the river Aulne. Riding, cycling and walking conditions are ideal with bridle-paths and marked footpaths. There is good fishing in rivers and lakes; also canoeing, boating and canal-cruising. Occasionally you can still hear the Breton language spoken in the more remote parts of the country and among the fishermen. Due to its cut-off position Finistère has also kept alive many of the old crafts and customs. Lace headdresses are still worn in the Bigouden area, and at *fêtes* and religious festivals Breton music accompanies processions, marches and dances in traditional costumes. While not as rich in prehistoric monuments as the Morbihan, the district includes some menhirs, such as the site at Lagat-Jar with its 143 standing stones. Important architectural features of Finistère are the famous *enclos paroissaux* (parish closes) which have fascinated visitors for centuries. These are old walled churches (mostly 16th and 17th-century) which include within their precincts all or some of the following – a triumphal arch, a cemetery, an ossuary, a calvary with sculptured figures and a fountain.

Of the larger towns, Morlaix on the north coast makes a good base for touring the beautiful countryside, the west Finistère coast, the parish closes and for sailing in the bay. Quimper, set on the river Odet on the south coast, is simply not to be missed. Its superb Gothic cathedral is set in the beautiful old quarter of the town which is criss-crossed by bridges in the style of Venice.

TOWNS AND RESORTS OF INTEREST (Finistère)

Audierne (35 km west of Quimper)

A small fishing-town set in the Goyen estuary below a wooded hill. There is a good beach one kilometre from the port. Boat trips are available to the Ile-de-Sein.

Beg-Meil (21 km south-east of Quimper)
Small sheltered resort with palm trees, mimosa and pine-covered sand dunes. Nearby Cap-Coz and Mousterlin also have safe beaches of fine sand. Take a boat trip across the bay to the medieval walled town of Concarneau or to the Iles-de-Glénan.

Bénodet (16 km south of Quimper)
Situated at the mouth of the beautiful Odet river, this is the most popular of the small, family, seaside resorts in Finistère and a yachting centre of international renown. Comparatively unspoilt, it offers the full range of accommodation, restaurants, etc., and a good selection of sporting facilities and holiday pursuits. There are two main beaches where children can play happily in the sand, children's swimming and beach clubs, two sailing and windsurfing schools, regattas, also boat, yacht and bicycle hire, tennis courts and hydrotherapy centre. This is also a good base for inland walking tours of the wooded countryside. Sea and river trips. 9- and 18-hole golf courses nearby.

Brest (71 km north-west of Quimper)
Modern city and large naval port with extensive dockyards and vast industrialized areas. For reasons of strict security only French citizens are allowed to visit the naval base. Interesting features include a 15th-century castle, a naval museum and a local-history museum. A variety of sea trips are available, all leaving from the Port de Commerce (along the coast to the Islands of Ouessant and Molène, etc). Also tours of the surrounding countryside. For breathtaking scenery and outstanding views of land and sea visit the

Pointe de Corsen and the Pointe de St-Mathieu west of Brest.

Camaret-sur-Mer (43 km north-west of Châteaulin)
Delightful old fishing-port set at the tip of the Crozon peninsula. The beach is of sand and shingle and swimming around here can be dangerous but there is a pretty yacht harbour, a 17th-century castle built by Vauban, a 16th-century chapel and a naval museum. Nearby at Lagat-Jar is a prehistoric site with 143 standing stones, at Pointe de Penhir the rocky cliffs rise to over 200 feet and at Pointe des Espangols there is a bird sanctuary. Boat excursions to a variety of locations include Tas des Pois bird sanctuary.

Carantec (15 km north-west of Morlaix)
Holiday resort and excellent little shopping town typical of many dotted all along the northern coast. Sandy beaches and secluded little coves may be found all around the peninsula and several small islands are within walking distance.

Châteaulin (29 km north of Quimper)
Small country town cut through by the river Aulne. Good fishing – salmon and trout. Cycle championships each September. Castle ruins and 16th-century chapel. Cruising on the river.

Concarneau (24 km south-east of Quimper)
Seaside resort and large fishing port with its wonderful medieval walled town set apart on an island reached by a causeway. Sandy beaches, museums and boat trips across the bay to Beg-Meil, also the Iles-de-Glénan (lighthouse, old fort, sailing school and bird sanctuary). Fishing museum and good shopping for antiques, pottery and curios. Colourful International Folk Festival in August – *Fête des Filets Bleus*. Rather crowded in high summer.

Douarnenez (22 km north-west of Quimper)

Large fishing-port and since 1945 has merged with its neighbours Ploaré, Pouldavid and Tréboul to form one large seaside resort. Good beaches and pleasure craft harbour. Wonderful walks around *quais*, through old streets and along coastal paths. Numerous inland excursions leave from here, also sea trips. The Thalassotherapy Centre here offering health treatments is open all year round. Visit the fish auction where you will more than likely hear Breton spoken, the church of Ploaré, Chapels of Ste-Hélène and St-Michel, the Laënnec Gardens and boat museum.

Le Faou (12 km north of Châteaulin)
Picturesque little harbour village worth a visit for its unusual 16th-century slate-fronted houses and riverside church with its Renaissance belfry.

La Forêt-Fouesnant (16 km south-east of Quimper)
Small, heavily wooded resort set in a very sheltered position at the head of a bay offering the combined pleasures of both sea and country. 9-hole golf course, 16th-century church and calvary.

Fouesnant (15 km south-east of Quimper)
Set by the sea and surrounded by apple orchards, this little town is famous for its cider and traditional Breton costume. Visit it in late July for the annual *fête* when you can enjoy both. A number of good sandy beaches surround the resort and the area is very sheltered with sand dunes and wooded paths. 9-hole golf course nearby.

Huelgoat (29 km south of Morlaix)
Built around a lake on the side of Mont d'Arrée, the setting of wooded hills, huge masses of granite rocks and rushing streams is superb. Rich in myths and legends, many relating to King Arthur, his knights and ladies, this is a romantic location with even a famous well-worn lovers walk – *Sentier des Amoureux*. In the town square stands a 16th-century church.

Landerneau (20 km east of Brest)
An estuary port with its town built on either side of the river
Elhorn. Linking the two sides is the Pont de Rohan. Built in
1510 it is reputed to be the oldest inhabited bridge in
Europe with its two rows of ancient houses and even a small
manor swaying above the river. The 16th-century church of
St-Thomas-de-Cantorbéry has a splendid bell tower and
carved rood screen. 9- and 18-hole golf courses at nearby St-
Urbain.

Landivisiau (22 km west of Morlaix)
Small market town with church dating back to the 1550s
and a 15th-century fountain. Near to the parish closes of
Lampaul-Guimiliau, Guimiliau and St-Thégonnec.

Locquirec (20 km north-east of Morlaix)
Pretty little fishing-port and lively resort with sandy
beaches. A good touring centre for exploring coastal and
inland areas.

Locronan (17 km north-west of Quimper)
Ancient little granite stone town very popular with tourists.
Its lovely town square with a well in the centre is enclosed
by beautifully preserved Renaissance houses. There are two
ancient churches to visit, a small folk museum and craft
workshops and sales rooms.

Loctudy (26 km south-west of Quimper)
Small fishing-port and resort set at the mouth of the Pont-
l'Abbé river. Its Romanesque church is said to be the best
preserved in Brittany. Boat trips to the offshore islands.

Morgat (37 km west of Châteaulin)
Small resort with fine sands near the west end of the Crozon
peninsula. Nearby are the Grandes Grottes. These caves can
be visited by boat.

Morlaix (25 km south-east of Roscoff)

Set deep in its river valley this ancient town still retains many old cobbled streets with half-timbered houses, pillared porches and inner courtyards. There are a local museum and churches to visit, pleasant river walks and tours of the town.

Plouescat (15 km west of St-Pol-de-Léon)
Attractive little town with a 16th-century covered market, its roof supported by huge carved beams.

Plougastel-Daoulas (11 km east of Brest)
Charming capital of the Plougastel peninsula and famous for its splendid calvary group, consisting of 180 figures, situated by the town's church.

Pont-Aven (17 km west of Quimperlé)
Located in the beautiful Aven valley this small town became famous as the place where Paul Gauguin headed a group of artists to found the Pont-Aven School of Art. Lots of galleries and an art museum to visit.

Pont-l'Abbé (20 km south-west of Quimper)
Capital of the Bigouden area, this little riverside town is well known for its lace and traditional headdresses. The 14th-century château houses a museum. Good market.

Quimper (72 km south-east of Brest)
Capital of Finistère and of the Cornouaille, this gem of a town is not to be missed. Sometimes referred to as 'The Venice of Brittany', numerous little bridges span the river Odet which runs through its centre. There are marvellous shops, cafés, restaurants and a wonderful old medieval quarter with a towering Gothic cathedral. Each July the great Celtic Festival attracts participants from all over Europe. During this festival the traditional costumes and headdresses of all the cantons of Brittany are on display. Visit the local potteries, art galleries and museums. Regular boat services down the river to Bénodet.

Quimperlé (44 km east of Quimper)
Quaint little town with old houses at its centre and an
unusual 11th-century round church.

Roscoff (28 km north-west of Morlaix)
Ferry port and charming town of grey granite buildings and
well known for its sea-water therapy centres
(Thalassotherapy). This is also a fine little holiday resort in
its own right. (See section on BRETON PORTS).

Rosporden (22 km east of Quimper)
Standing by a lake formed by the river Aven, this little
country town has a church dating from the 14th century.

Ste-Anne-la-Palud (7 km north-west of Douarnenez)
Famous for its tiny chapel where one of the best known
Breton *pardons* is held at the end of August each year.

St-Pol-de-Léon (5 km south of Roscoff)
Sitting among market gardens this small ancient cathedral
city is built on a plateau near the Bay of Morlaix. 16th- and
17th-century houses with unusual shutters and turrets are to
be found in the old area between the 13th-century cathedral
and the 14th-century Chapelle du Kreisker.

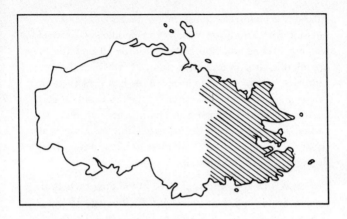

ILLE-ET-VILAINE

Bounded by the beautiful, wild and rugged Côte d'Eméraude, with its ever-green sea, cliffs, rocky points and stretches of fine sand, several towns along here are popular as holiday centres. Dinard, the largest and most sophisticated – palm trees, plush hotels and grand villas – offers the full range of amenities and, despite its grandeur, accommodation to suit every taste and budget. The other small coastal towns, such as Cancale, St-Briac and St-Lunaire, with their good beaches and spectacular views, are suitable for quiet, family holidays. The ancient Corsaire port of St-Malo, with its exciting and swashbuckling past was badly bombed in the last war. Since then, however, the old walled town has been magnificently restored to its former 18th-century glory and presents a wonderful sight to those sailing into its harbour. Flanked on either side by the attractive little resorts of St-Servan and Paramé (now part of greater St-Malo) it makes one of the largest tourist centres in Brittany.

Inland, the country of forest, moors, lakes, and fields bursting with artichokes, onions and cauliflowers, is ideal for walking, cycling and riding. Ancient little villages and towns are full of character and have changed little over the centuries – medieval Vitré is one of the best preserved in France and old feudal communities such as Combourg, Châteaugiron and Fougères still huddle beneath their castles. The landscape is dotted with churches, chapels and crosses at road junctions – like those at Champeaux, Dol-de-Bretagne, Les Iffs and Redon.

To the west lies the beautiful forest of Paimpont where the ancient druids had their university. Rich in legends relating to King Arthur and the Knights of the Round Table, Lancelot and Guinevere and Merlin the wizard, who are said to have lived here, references to them are found in local place names. Historically a frontier with the rest of France, the eastern part of the Department is strung across with nineteen castles and monuments open to the public. There are some 300 prehistoric megaliths in this area – standing stones, enclosures and cairns. A large number are located at St-Just in the south. The *Roche-aux-Fées* (Fairy Rock) near Essé has forty-three huge stones and chambers.

Cut through by waterways, the Department takes its name from its two main rivers, the Ille and the Vilaine, and canal and river cruising offer an alternative way of travelling. You can, for example, hire a cabin cruiser at St-Malo, meander down to Nantes, then cruise right through Brittany all the way to Brest.

Ille-et-Vilaine makes an ideal base for visiting other places, such as Mont-St-Michel the famous abbey island, the Normandy landing beaches and the Loire Valley.

TOWNS AND RESORTS OF INTEREST (Ille-et-Vilaine)

Antrain (24 km south of Mont-St-Michel)
Little market town set at the point where the Couesnon and the Loisance rivers meet. Dating back to the 11th century it has some old buildings in its narrow, steep streets. Nearby are several castles to visit.

Bain-de-Bretagne (32 km south of Rennes)
Lovely little town by a lake between Nantes and Rennes and a good stopping point. 17th-century chapel of Coudray just outside.

Bécherel (31 km north-west of Rennes)
A hill-top village with some very old houses and with extensive views over the surrounding countryside. Nearby Caradeuc and Couëlan castles have beautiful gardens and the fine 17th-century château of Montmuran is open to the public. At Les Iffs the little parish church dates back to the 14th century.

Bruz (6 km south of Rennes)
The delightful town square here has an unusual church of rose-veined schist, pine trees and a weeping willow.

Cancale (14.5 km east of St-Malo)
Typical small fishing-port just across the bay from the famous monastery island of Mont-St-Michel. Cancale is famous throughout France for its top-quality oysters. These are featured in hotels, restaurants, bars and even street stalls. A good touring base for both the beautiful Côte d'Eméraude and inland areas. Lovely cliff walks.

Châteaugiron (16 km south-east of Rennes)
Neat little town with a medieval castle and streets of ancient houses sloping down below. *Son-et-Lumière* in the summer.

Combourg (37 km north of Rennes)

The great, gloomy castle here with its dark spires and turrets rising above the trees was the childhood home of the famous French writer Chateaubriand. Built in 1016 it is set on a rocky hill overlooking the lake and pretty little town.

Dinard (22 km north of Dinan)
One of the main holiday resorts in these parts, it is beautifully sited in the Rance estuary within sight of the ramparts of St-Malo. Sheltered from the west winds it has been popular since the Americans and British discovered it in the 1850s. Dinard still retains much of its old-world atmosphere with its broad promenade above golden sands, grand hotels and large villas set among fig and palm trees and colourful profusions of exotic flowers. Less exclusive than in Victorian times, today it offers accommodation and amenities to suit all tastes and budgets. The full range of sports and leisure facilities is available. It has three good beaches flanked by rocky bays, two large seawater pools, an eighteen-hole golf course, tennis courts, sailing and windsurfing schools, a riding centre, casino, discos and a sea aquarium museum. There is also a small aerodrome and flying club.

Dol-de-Bretagne (24 km south-east of St-Malo)
An ancient cathedral town and agricultural centre with some interesting 17th-century buildings and some of the oldest houses in the whole of France. The local-history museum is worth a visit, also one-hour tour of the town. 18-hole golf course nearby. On the Epiniac road (a few miles south-east of Dol) is a prehistoric site with a 31-foot high standing stone.

Fougères (48 km north of Rennes)
Built on two levels the modern town sits on a hill while below in a valley lies the medieval town with its many towered feudal castle – one of the largest in Europe, a Gothic church and narrow, sloping streets of ancient houses.

Good shopping, beautiful gardens partly located on the town's ramparts, town and castle tours and a shoe museum. Three kilometres away in Fougères forest are several megalithic monuments.

La Guerche-de-Bretagne (22 km south of Vitré)
At the centre of this attractive little country town the square is edged with some interesting old houses, their upper storeys supported by heavy wooden columns, and a 13th-century church with beautifully carved choir-stalls and stained-glass. Grand festival each year on the Feast of the Assumption (15 August) when a 17th-century Madonna is carried in procession. About ten miles away the *Roche-aux-Fées* (Fairy Rock) is one of the finest megalithic sites in Brittany with forty-two standing stones, some of them weighing around 40 tons, and chambers.

Hédé (22 km north of Rennes)
Set on a hill and overlooking a dramatic series of locks of the Ille-et-Rance canal and a lake on the other side, this pretty little village has beautiful hanging gardens, some old houses, a 16th-century church and the ruins of a feudal castle. Annual festival first fortnight in August with various cultural events including jazz and classical music concerts, dance and theatre.

Langon (20 km north-east of Redon)
Built on an old Roman way this town boasts the only Roman building still standing in this part of the world. Close by, the *Demoiselles de Langon* – thirty prehistoric stones – are dotted about in the quiet countryside. According to local legend these were young single girls who were turned to stone for preferring dancing to going to church.

Paimpont (40 km west of Rennes)
Set by a lake deep in the beautiful forest of Brocéliande, where according to legend Merlin worked his magic, this delightful little town has an abbey church at its centre which

dates back to the 7th century. The main street leading to the abbey is entered through an ancient archway.

Redon (65 km south-west of Rennes)
Placed at the crossing of the Vilaine and Nantes-Brest canal, this lively little market town has several 15th to 17th-century houses which grace the Grande Rue. The Basilica of St-Sauveur is unusual for its 13th-century tower which was cut off by fire in 1780 and now stands beside the church. Boat trips on the Vilaine.

Rennes (69 km south-east of St-Malo)
The capital of Brittany, this is also a cultural centre with two theatres and several concert halls. Its cathedral (Cathédrale-de-St-Pierre) restored in 1844 stands in the old quarter amid a network of narrow, ancient streets lined with crooked 15th- and 16th-century half-timbered houses. Most of the rest of the city was destroyed by fire in 1720 but many streets of graceful 18th-century granite houses add interest. Of the many gardens and parks the *Jardin du Thabbor* is outstanding. Covering twenty-five acres it dates right back to the middle ages. There are several museums – art, archaeology and local history. City tours and excursions and nearby are two 18-hole golf courses.

St-Briac-sur-Mer (24 km north of Dinan)
Small family seaside resort and fishing-port. Ideal for a quiet holiday with good beaches and an 18-hole golf course.

St-Lunaire (5 km west of Dinard)
Small but smart resort which was grown around the two sides of a peninsula. It has rocky points, two good beaches, spectacular views and lovely walks.

St-Malo (69 km north of Rennes)
Channel port of entry and resort. For full description see the section on BRETON PORTS in this book.

Vitré (36 km east of Rennes)

An ancient frontier town rising up above the Vilaine, this is one of the best-preserved medieval towns in France and simply must not be missed. Its fortress castle, rebuilt in the 14th and 15th centuries, overlooks a maze of narrow streets with lopsided, half-timbered houses and sloping cellar doors at street level. Nearby is the 15th-century Flamboyant Gothic church of Notre-Dame. The town is still partly surrounded by the old ramparts.

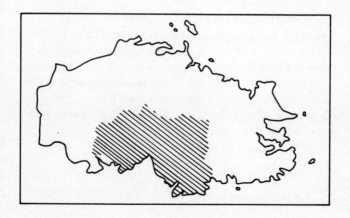

MORBIHAN

This department in Southern Brittany takes its name (little sea) from the Gulf of Morbihan which lies between Vannes and the Bay of Quiberon. Its attractions include a coastline of outstanding natural beauty indented by estuaries, rivers and inland waterways, fine sandy beaches and a string of seaside resorts such as Sarzeau, La Trinité-sur-Mer, Port-Louis and Quiberon. Offshore lie several beautiful islands, the best known being Belle-Ile-en-Mer. Its sheltered locality along with its inlets and islands, 6,000 mooring places and numerous sailing schools make it an ideal area for water sports particularly windsurfing and sailing. The Bay of Quiberon is the scene of many major European sailing championships, and transatlantic races often set sail from the port of Lorient.

Inland is mainly agricultural but there is plenty to see and do, be it walking, cycling or riding through the woodlands and gorse-covered moors, visiting the great châteaux of Josselin and Pontivy or sightseeing in the medieval city of Vannes. There are about a dozen lakeside water-sports centres for sailing, windsurfing, rowing, canoeing and waterskiing. Many have facilities for camping. With 260 kms of waterways winding their way through Morbihan, including part of the Nantes-Brest canal, it is not surprising that boating, barging and canal cruising are all popular holiday activities, as is angling, the rivers being rich in pike, perch and trout.

One of the greatest attractions of this area is undoubtably the megaliths. Mysterious symbols of religion, worship and death, their true purpose unknown, they are to be found here in one of the greatest concentrations in the world. Some standing over 60 feet tall, endless lines of these strange standing stones bear witness to a civilization that grew up in Brittany around 3500 BC. They can be seen not only at Carnac, the most famous site, but also along the length of the Morbihan coastline (often called the 'Megalith Coast') and on the Lanvaux moors.

Throughout the Department there is a rich heritage of architecture and monuments in which one can find evidence of the very many faiths practised over the centuries. Here in the dark forests and harsh moorlands originated the legends of Lancelot, Merlin and Morgane. Today, the Morbihan people still cling to deep-rooted traditions which are celebrated in their numerous religious, folk and music festivals.

The abundance of camellias, mimosa, rhododendrons, fig and palm trees seem to bear out the assertion that Morbihan, with its sheltered, southerly position, has a drier and more temperate climate than the other parts of Brittany, and has air and sea temperatures on average a couple of degrees higher than in the resorts along the north coast.

TOWNS AND RESORTS OF INTEREST (Morbihan)

Auray   (18 km west of Vannes)
An old town set on the banks of the river Auray. The
attractive ancient quarter of St-Goustan, which has been
mainly pedestrianized, has twisting narrow streets and
alleyways lined with picturesque 15th-century houses.
Benjamin Franklin gave his name to one of the quays: he
landed at Auray at the start of his mission to sign a treaty
with France. Across the 17th-century stone bridge is the Loc
Promenade with a shady path running up to the Loc
Ramparts from where there is an excellent view of the port
and oyster beds which line the estuary. The 17th-century
church of St-Gildas is at the top of the town. An 18-hole golf
course is nearby. Six kilometres north is the famous
sanctuary of Ste-Anne-d'Auray, scene of one of the best
known *pardons* in Brittany. The feast of Ste-Anne starts on 25
July and lasts two days.

Baud (25 km north of Auray)
A small town by the river Evel. Interesting wooden statues
in the church which, though modern, is attached to a 16th-
century chapel. It is perhaps best known for its statue, the
Venus de Quinipily, to be found about a mile away towards
Hennebont. Of Roman or Egyptian origin it became a cult
figure and object of worship in the 17th century. It was
twice torn down and thrown in the river by order of the
Church only to be retrieved by the peasants. It now stands
serenely by a fountain.

Belle-Ile-en-Mer (reached by boat from Quiberon)
This is the largest of Brittany's offshore islands and its
picturesque whitewashed houses and coastline of tiny creeks
and bays have always attracted artists, including Monet and
Matisse. The main town is Le Palais, which has a 16th-
century citadel, and the island is a centre for international

yachting events. Many megalithic monuments can be seen on the moorlands here, and what was formerly Sarah Bernhardt's farmhouse is now an 18-hole golf course.

Carnac (30 km south-west of Vannes)
The spectacular sight of thousands of prehistoric standing stones arranged in seemingly endless parallel lines and semi-circles has made Carnac famous throughout the world. Outstanding examples of these mysterious formations, the alignments of Menec, Kermario and Kerlescan, are to be found to the north of the town. Also worth visiting is the St-Michel Tumulus, a huge mound of stones and earth over burial chambers. At the top of the mount stands a small chapel and the view of the megaliths from here is superb. The excellent museum founded by a Scot, J. Miln, is a wonderful source of information on ancient Brittany. The town of Carnac is pleasant with a 17th-century church and an attractive main square. At the south end of the town can be found one of the finest beaches in Brittany making Carnac-Plage a popular seaside resort. From here there are good views of the islands and the Quiberon peninsula. There are 9- and 18-hole golf courses 7 kms away.

Le Faouët (40 km north of Lorient)
A peaceful country town built around an enormous 16th-century timber covered market. Within a few kilometres are three superb chapels, Ste-Barbe, St-Fiacre and St-Nicolas, all worth visiting not only for their fine interiors and ancient carvings but also for their beautiful settings.

La Gacilly (55 km north-east of Vannes)
It has good reason to call itself a *cité fleurie*. From April to October masses of brightly coloured flowers spill from hanging-baskets and window-boxes throughout the town. It is also a centre for weaving, pottery, sculpture and other arts and crafts.

Hennebont (10 km north of Lorient)
Built on the banks of the wide river Blavet this walled town
was very badly damaged during the Second World War but
parts of the ramparts and fortified city gate remain. In the
vast Place du Maréchal-Foch stands the 16th-century
Gothic church of Notre-Dame de Paradis with its enormous
belfry and steeple 72 metres in height. A famous stud farm is
located in the grounds of the ruined Abbaye de la Joie.

Josselin (42 km north-east of Vannes)
Centred round what is probably the best known castle in
Brittany, its massive fortress walls and three great circular
pointed towers reflected in the river Oust, Josselin is a
charming town with 16th- and 17th-century houses lining
the narrow streets. Within the walls of the castle is a richly
decorated and ornamented dwelling-house facing a
courtyard. Built by the powerful Rohan family around 1500
(members of the family still live here today), the luxurious
ground-floor rooms which were restored in the 19th century
are on view to the public.

A great *pardon* is held every September at Josselin at the
Basilica of Our Lady of the Rosebush (Notre-Dame-de-
Roncier). It gets its name from the 9th-century legend of the
peasant who discovered a statue of the Virgin while cutting
brambles in his field. No matter how many times it was
removed the statue always reappeared on the same spot
where eventually a sanctuary was built. Only fragments of
the statue remain today.

In a field half-way between Josselin and Ploërmel a stone
pyramid marks the spot of the 14th-century 'Battle of the
Thirty'. During the War of Succession the Breton
commander of the garrison at Josselin, Jean de Beaumanoir,
and the leader of the opposing English mercenaries, Robert
Bemborough, agreed that thirty knights from each side
should battle it out on foot using swords, daggers, battle-axes

and pikes. At the end of the day the English were either dead or taken prisoner with victory going to Josselin.

Larmor-Plage (6 km south of Lorient)
Small seaside resort with lovely beaches and 16th-century church with fine altarpiece and frescos. Travelling west from Larmor the peaceful coast road passes through several tiny family resorts all of which have marvellous views out to sea and to the Island of Groix.

Locmariaquer (13 km south of Auray)
A small holiday resort best known for the megaliths in the surrounding country which include the *Grand Menhir*, one of the largest in the world, and the *Table des Marchands*, one of the most famous. There are boat trips from here around the Bay of Morbihan and along the Auray river.

Lorient (48 km west of Vannes)
Created as the Port de l'Orient in the 17th century by the French East India Company, Lorient is a major commercial port. Over 80% of the town was destroyed in bombing raids between 1940 and 1944 and it has since been almost totally rebuilt. Modern, somewhat characterless buildings line wide boulevards and a pedestrian shopping area centres around the bustling Place Aristide-Briand. An outstanding example of modern design is the church of Notre-Dame-de-Victoire in the Place Alsace-Lorraine. The busy, colourful fishing-port of Keroman is best visited in the morning when scores of trawlers unload their catch. There are several nearby seaside resorts and boat trips to the islands of Belle-Ile and Groix leave from the Quai de l'Estacade. Lorient also plays a part in the revival of Breton culture, hosting an important Celtic festival every August.

Malestroit (35 km north-east of Vannes)
Old town in a pleasant setting by the river Oust with lovely canalside walks. It has many medieval timbered houses displaying interesting and amusing sculptures and carvings.

The 12th-century church was considerably enlarged during the 16th century, and of particular note is the panelled south doorway flanked by animal statues.

Ploërmel (46 km north-east of Vannes)

In this small town, scene of many battles in the 14th and 16th centuries, are to be found many well preserved medieval houses. In the Rue Beaumanoir stands the former home of the Dukes of Brittany. The Gothic church named after St Armel who founded the town in the 6th century, has eight magnificent stained-glass windows and remarkable carvings on the north doorway. Of much interest is the town's 19th-century astronomical clock, which gives the time worldwide. There are pleasant walks by the nearby lake, the Etang du Duc, which also attracts fishermen and windsurfers.

Pontivy (52 km north of Vannes)

At the end of the 18th century Napoleon decided that Pontivy was in an excellent position strategically, lying half-way along the Nantes-Brest canal which he was then having built. He developed the town, laying it out along strict geometrical lines, and built a town hall, school and barracks. It was renamed 'Napoléonville' but reverted to Pontivy after the fall of the Empire. The old town is in complete contrast with the 15th-and 16th-century half-timbered houses in the narrow streets around the Gothic church of Notre-Dame-de-la-Joie. Pontivy originally grew up around the massive walls, ramparts and bastion towers of the 15th-century Château de Rohan which has recently been extensively restored.

Port-Louis (29 km west of Auray)

Built on the estuary of the Scorff and Blavet rivers, Port-Louis is a small fishing port and seaside resort popular with the inhabitants of Lorient on the opposite bank. This former fortified town still has its 17th-century ramparts and citadel which now houses a museum.

Quiberon (46 km south-west of Vannes)
Set at the southernmost tip of the 15-kilometre-long
peninsula of the same name, Quiberon has a huge, sandy
beach, a busy marina and one of the largest thalassotherapy
centres in France. It also has a sardine fishing-port (Port-
Maria) from where one can take boat trips to the islands.
The paths along the cliff top of the western coast known as
the 'Côte Sauvage' are ideal for invigorating walks. Below,
the turbulent sea crashes against rocky crevices, caves and
tiny, sandy beaches. Swimming is very dangerous here.
From the Pointe de Conguel at the south-east end of the
peninsula there are lovely views over the bay to Belle-Ile and
Houat (18-hole golf course at the former). Around 100,000
visitors come to Quiberon every year so be prepared for
slow-moving traffic on the main peninsula road during the
peak months.

La Roche-Bernard (40 km south-east of Vannes)
A picturesque old town standing on a headland overlooking
the Vilaine river. In the Ruicard quarter some attractive
15th and 16th-century wooden houses survive from the days
when La Roche was important for its shipbuilding. Nearby,
an impressive new suspension bridge crosses the river.

Rochefort-en-Terre (34 km east of Vannes)
A delightful, small fortified town built on a rocky
promontory surrounded by woods, ravines and orchards.
Geraniums grow in profusion in the window-boxes of the
lovely 17th-century granite houses. There are numerous
antique shops to browse around and the 12th to 16th-
century church has interesting stalls and a Renaissance
altarpiece with painted statues.

St-Gildas-de-Rhuys (38 km south of Vannes)
A small town on the Rhuys peninsula with several excellent
beaches nearby. A monastery was founded here by St Gildas
in the 6th century. Its most famous abbot was the

philosopher Abélard in the 12th century. In his letters to his
love Héloïse he tells of his hatred for the remote,
inhospitable countryside and wild coastline. The church was
mainly rebuilt during the 16th and 17th centuries. Behind
the high altar is located the tomb of St Gildas and the
treasury contains a valuable collection of shrines and relics.
There is an 18-hole golf course at the tip of the peninsula at
Le Crouesty.

Sarzeau (36 km south of Vannes)
The main town on the Rhuys peninsula, it has some well
preserved 17th-century granite houses with decorated
window-frames. Nearby is the Château of Kerlévenan built
in the 18th century in Italian style. Not far in the other
direction stands the great Château de Suscinio which was
the summer residence of the Dukes of Brittany in the Middle
Ages. This restored fortress is an impressive sight standing on
a wild, windswept site by the sea.

La Trinité-sur-Mer (28 km south-west of Vannes)
A popular, small seaside resort with a long sandy beach and
a sheltered yacht harbour considered to be one of the best on
the Atlantic coast. The town is built on a slope leading down
to the Crach estuary where oyster beds nestle in the tidal
flats. Cross the Kerisper bridge for a lovely view of the
estuary and port.

Vannes (48 km east of Lorient)
A busy agricultural town at the top of the Gulf of Morbihan,
Vannes is of immense interest and should not be missed. The
massive medieval ramparts have been extremely well
preserved and it is possible to walk along a considerable part
of them. Looking down on the moat below one is greeted
with the colourful sight of elaborately laid out flower-beds.
From here, too, there is a good view of the restored wash-
houses where centuries ago the women of the town did their
communal laundry. Behind the ramparts lies the medieval

town, now largely pedestrianized, thus making it easier to stroll round the narrow twisting streets with their half-timbered houses, ancient buildings, antique shops and boutiques. The Place Henri 1V is particularly interesting and nearby is the Gothic Cathedral St-Pierre which has many treasures exhibited in the old chapter-house. Other attractions of Vannes include its fine public garden, the archaeology museum, the large aquarium and the port from where there are boat trips round the Gulf.

FOOD AND DRINK

FOOD

Lobsters, prawns, shrimps, oysters, crabs, in fact every kind of seafood, and brought to the table only hours after the catch. Do try a *plateau de fruits de mer* but allow a couple of hours to get through it! Pork and chicken are of excellent quality as are locally grown cauliflowers and artichokes. *Crêpes* are thin pancakes stuffed with sweet or savoury fillings (*galettes* are similar but made with buckwheat) and Brittany is famous for its mouth-watering *pâtisseries*, butter cakes and biscuits. The strawberries of Plougastel-Daoulas have a flavour all of their own.

DRINK

Cider is usually drunk with *crêpes*, and Muscadet or Gros-Plant, the fine white wines of the Nantes area, are perfect with seafood. Plougastel strawberry liqueur is delightful after a meal.

RESTAURANTS

By law restaurants must display their menus outside, so study these and remember that it is always a good idea to choose a restaurant popular with French diners. Although you may select from the *à la carte* menu, the *table d'hôte* menus, of which there are usually a few, are much better value. You will find that four or five course meals are comparatively reasonably priced. Children are welcomed and it is not necessary to order a full meal for them. If you wish, you may pay a nominal sum for a *couvert* (place setting) and let the child share your food. A list of restaurants may be obtained in France at local tourist offices. (For addresses, look under TOURIST OFFICES and LOISIRS ACCUEIL booking service.) In the U.K. write to the French Government Tourist Office (178 Piccadilly, London, W1V) enclosing a S.A.E.
See also EATING OUT in the PRACTICAL INFORMATION section.

HOW TO GET THERE

BY AIR

Direct flights from UK to Brest, Dinard, Lannion, Lorient, Morlaix, Nantes, Quimper, Rennes and St-Brieuc. Also flights via Paris. (See also AIR TRAVEL in the Practical Information section.)

BY RAIL

Rail services to all the major towns. Links to St-Brieuc and Lannion from St-Malo and Roscoff. Also from Paris via Rennes. TGV (High Speed Trains) now run as far as Brest in the west and Le Croisic in the south.

BY CAR FERRY

Direct to the Breton ports of Roscoff and St-Malo from the UK and Ireland or to other French channel ports. (See FERRY COMPANIES in the Practical Information section.)

ROAD TRAVEL

Good network of major and secondary roads including several stretches of motorway. Recommended map – Michelin 230 which details the whole of Brittany. (See also DRIVING in the Practical Information section.)

THE BRETON PORTS

On disembarking, most travellers hurry from the ferry
terminal to the railway stations or major roads that will take
them to their holiday destination. In this section we have
tried to describe the ports as somewhere to spend that first or
last day in Brittany. With the wide range of attractions they
have to offer, it may be that you will be tempted to stay
longer.

SAINT-MALO

If your first sight of France is Saint-Malo you couldn't wish
for anything more impressive. The coves of fine sand and
marinas, lined with splendid yachts, are dominated by the
ancient granite walled city that faces the sea and the estuary
of the Rance. Within its fortified walls lie a maze of narrow
streets, winding passageways, flagged courtyards, and tall
gabled houses which, though badly damaged in the last war,
have been totally rebuilt in 17th- and 18th-century style.
The visitor may stroll at leisure in the pedestrian precinct,
browsing round the antique shops or studying the menus
outside the picturesque restaurants and *crêperies*. In the
summer, street musicians and entertainers are often to be
found performing in the cobbled squares. The castle (Bastille
de l'Ouest) houses a waxworks and a museum dedicated to
the history of the town and its most famous citizens,
including Jacques Cartier who discovered Canada. From its
watchtowers, as indeed from the ramparts, there are
panoramic views of the Bay of Saint-Malo, the offshore
islands and the river Rance. At high tide the waves dash
against the ramparts and at low tide you can walk to the
Iles de Grand Bé.

Saint-Malo and the adjoining resort of Paramé can also offer the visitor sheltered beaches for safe swimming, water sports, children's clubs, sailing, underwater diving schools, two yacht harbours, an aquarium, riding clubs, tennis and squash courts, horse-racing, golf, a casino, an olympic sized swimming-pool, hypermarkets, thermal baths and Thalassotherapy centre.

Neighbouring St-Servan is a busy little town with a good market and pleasant walks along the cliffs. There are day excursions by hydrofoil to Jersey and Guernsey and boat trips to the Iles de Chausey and Cap Fréhel, a natural reserve for birds, which rises to 70 metres above sea level. Trips, too, along the river Rance as far as Dinan, a very attractive medieval town with 600-year-old ramparts and a pretty yacht harbour. Also within easy travelling distance along the coast is the elegant resort of Dinard with its palm-lined streets and luxury hotels and in the other direction Cancale, renowned for its oyster beds.

Further information, contact:-

Office de Tourisme,
Esplanade Saint-Vincent,
35400 Saint-Malo

ROSCOFF

Although in recent years Roscoff has become the arrival and departure point for the cross-channel ferries that sail to and from Plymouth and Cork, the town itself – only two minutes from the Gare Maritime – has remained unspoilt with its charming old streets, elegant houses and hotels and an interesting Gothic church, Notre-Dame-De-Kroaz-Baz, which has a tall Renaissance tower. For the visitor there are pleasant walks round the town, an aquarium, small shops selling Breton pottery and paintings, *crêperies* and very good restaurants, many with dining-rooms overlooking the sea. Try a Breton speciality or *plateau de fruits de mer*. Although the beaches at Roscoff are mainly shingle, good beaches (often deserted) are to be found only fifteen minutes away by regular boat service on the delightful Ile de Batz, its coastline dominated by a tall lighthouse. The residents here are mainly involved in fishing, seaweed collecting and market gardening.

The healthy invigorating climate of this corner of Brittany attracts visitors in large numbers. Renowned as a health spa since the last century, Roscoff has many health centres and clinics offering treatments based on sea water and thermal baths. It is also a town well known in the field of Marine Biology with an extensive research station. Set in the fertile countryside of North Finistère, the surrounding fields of cauliflowers, onions and artichokes stretch for mile upon mile. The export of these vegetables to the UK brought about the formation of Brittany Ferries sailing between Roscoff and Plymouth. But Roscoff has always had strong historical links with England and Scotland. In 1548 the five-year-old Mary Queen of Scots landed here for her engagement to the French Dauphin and the house where she is supposed to have lived can still be seen. Bonnie Prince Charlie is also said to have landed here, fleeing from the English after his defeat at Culloden.

Between Roscoff and Perros-Guirec, explore the fascinating Côte de Granit Rose, a wild, rocky coastline of pink granite, isolated headlands, sheer cliffs and sandy inlets. Just five minutes from Roscoff is St-Pol-de-Léon, a beautiful town with wide squares and busy markets. Long before you get there you will spot the 15th-century bell tower of the Chapelle de Notre-Dame-du-Kreisker. 77 metres high and with lovely open-work spires and pinnacles, it can be seen from miles around. St-Pol also has a twin-spired Gothic cathedral with exquisitely carved stalls and 16th-century stained-glass windows. Stroll along the riverside and enjoy the lovely views over the estuary. A little further away is Morlaix, a lively, commercial town with good shops, a hypermarket, an old quarter with medieval houses and a splendid, pink granite viaduct above the town centre.

Further information, contact:-

Office of Tourism,
Chapelle Sainte-Anne,
BP 40, 29680, Roscoff.

ACCOMMODATION

HOTELS

French hotels are graded from one to four star plus de-luxe. Prices are by the room – displayed at reception and in the room itself. Ask to see the room as this is common practice in France. Breakfast, continental style, is almost always priced separately. If you want to book full or half-board for more than a few days you will be able to take advantage of a special reduced rate (*pension* or *demi-pension*). Motorists should have little difficulty in finding overnight accommodation as there are hundreds of small well-run hotels throughout the region. However, in the height of the season coastal resorts and tourist centres should be avoided; start looking no later than four in the afternoon. Hotels will not hold room reservations after 6 pm without a deposit. Many hotels expect you to take dinner so the menu, displayed outside, may be a consideration in the choice of your hotel.

At the top end of the scale are the châteaux hotels. The word château is used somewhat loosely in this context to describe grand houses, manor houses and rather large old buildings usually in inland settings, with tennis courts, riding and fishing facilities, etc. What the term generally denotes is beautiful surroundings, comfort, excellent cuisine and first-class service. But be prepared to pay for it.

Logis et Auberges de France is a chain of small, hospitable, owner-run hotels offering excellent value for money – comfortable rooms and moderately priced meals which often include Breton specialities. Look out for their green-and-yellow sign depicting a hearth and chimney.

Local Tourist Offices (*Syndicats d'Initiative*) will help with information and reservations. They can also book *Chambre d'Hôtes* accommodation – bed and breakfast in private homes or guest houses.

Many British tour operators offer hotel-based holidays with all the types of hotels already mentioned and/or reservation services for overnight stops or 'go as you please' arrangements. See listings TOUR OPERATORS. For individual hotels see listings HOTELS.

APARTMENTS, GITES AND VILLAS

Self-catering accommodation is widely available throughout Brittany. Clients may rent the property and make their own travel arrangements or book a package holiday through a tour operator to include reduced air or ferry fares in the deal. The word 'villa' is usually, but not always, employed to describe houses at the coast or near to the sea. The word '*gîte*' is a blanket term used for rural properties ranging from small dwellings to farm houses or manor houses. These are often located a mile or two from the nearest town. Apartments in country houses may also be called '*gîtes*'. All have modern amenities, electricity and flush toilets. Bed linen and towels are not normally provided. Enquire about extra charges – e.g., for gas, electricity, water. Usually a returnable deposit is required against breakages. Self-catering studios are also available in holiday villages and seaside resorts where one can generally find plenty of leisure and sports facilities.

For further information on booking this type of holiday in Brittany contact the Regional Tourist Office or Loisirs Accueil. See listings – TOURIST OFFICES and LOISIRS ACCUEIL. A brochure can be obtained from the London

office of
   Gites de France,
   178 Piccadilly,
   London. W1V 9DB.
   Tel: 071 493 3480 or 408 1343.

Several British tour operators also offer self-catering holidays
in Brittany. See listings TOUR OPERATORS.

CAMPING/CARAVANNING

The popularity of this type of holiday is undoubtably due to
the number and quality of French campsites. Officially
graded one to four stars, at the bottom end of the range you
will find very basic facilities which increase and improve as
you go up the ratings. On a four-star site you would expect
to find a beautifully landscaped campsite with lots of trees
and flowers, the *emplacements* (pitches) divided by hedgerows,
and made-up roads often lit at night. Among the excellent
amenities will be a bar, restaurant and/or 'take-away' meals
service, fully tiled showers, and toilet blocks, laundry room,
games room, children's play area, shop or supermarket and
often a swimming-pool. At the very top end of the range are
campsites carrying the CASTEL-CAMPING name – top
quality sites in the grounds of châteaux and manor houses in
outstandingly beautiful locations. On smaller sites many of
the facilities are open only during July and August. The
nightly rate varies according to the grading and facilities
provided. Many of the larger sites hire out chalets, luxury
mobile homes and fully equipped ready-erected tents large
enough for six people. These, too, are available through
British tour operators, who as part of a package will also
arrange your transport – self drive or by coach. If touring
with your own tent or caravan, be warned that in July and
August seaside sites near good beaches are very busy so start
looking late morning, the time when departing campers are

likely to be leaving. Or book in advance through one of the British companies who specialize in making these types of reservations.

N.B. Never camp on private land without first asking permission. *Camping Sauvage* (wild camping) is forbidden in forests and National Parks. However, farm camping (*Camping à la Ferme*) is usually available with a maximum of six *emplacements*, basic washing and toilet facilities; also small country sites (*Aires Naturelles de Camping*) with a maximum of twenty-five *emplacements* and basic facilities.

A camping carnet, available from camping organizations in the UK entitles you to a discount on some sites. Not necessary if you book through a tour operator.

In Brittany local Tourist Offices will provide full information on campsites or make reservations for your own tent or caravan. For an inclusive camping/caravanning holiday book through a British tour operator. See listings – TOUR OPERATORS.

For individual campsites see listings – CAMPSITES.

HOLIDAY VILLAGES

A holiday village is as its name suggests a self-contained village with holiday accommodation which can be bungalows, chalets or apartments built round a central area with a wide range of leisure facilities. Expect to find a club house, a bar, restaurant, supermarket, one or several swimming-pools, tennis and volley-ball courts, children's playground, bicycle hire shop and if not near a river, possibly a man-made lake for fishing. There may also be a children's club, on-site entertainers and regular programmes of water-sports, gymnastics and keep-fit sessions. It's a fun-type, family holiday in a relaxed atmosphere. For a list of these contact the Regional Tourist Office or Loisirs Accueil. See listings TOURIST OFFICES AND LOISIRS ACCUEIL.

Some British tour operators offer this type of holiday as a self-drive package deal. See listings — TOUR OPERATORS.

The following French companies offer accommodation in a wide range of holiday villages throughout France:

Leo Lagrange Loisirs,
17 Rue de la Grande-Batelière, 75009 Paris.

Villages Vacances Familles,
38 Boulevard Edgar-Quinet, 75014 Paris.

Occaj,
95 Rue d'Amsterdam, 75008 Paris.

YOUTH HOSTELS

Brittany is well supplied with youth hostels which offer inexpensive accommodation to young people of all nationalities. Grades range from the very small and simple to the large and more sophisticated. Some are open to handicapped persons in wheelchairs. Most also offer inclusive sports/special interest holidays or may alternatively be able to organize participation in local sports and activities. Bicycles are usually available for hire. For further information contact:

Association Bretonne des Auberges de Jeunesse,
La Haute Boë,
35133 Fleurigné.

In the UK contact:

   The Youth Hostels Association,
    14 Southampton Street,
    London WC2. Tel: 071 836 1036.

See also listings – YOUTH HOSTELS.

PRACTICAL INFORMATION

AIR TRAVEL

Within Brittany there are airports at Brest, Dinard, Lannion, Lorient, Morlaix, Nantes, Quimper, Rennes, and St-Brieuc.

For flights to Paris and/or Brittany contact – Air France, 158, New Bond Street, London W1Y OAY. Tel: 071 499 9511.

Air Inter: Contact Air France as above. Internal Domestic Service covering thirty French cities and towns including several in Brittany.

Brit Air: Tel: 0293 502044 or contact Air France as above. (Direct from Gatwick to Brest, Quimper and Rennes).

British Airways: (Personal Callers) 52 Grosvenor Gardens, Victoria, London SW1. Tel: 071 897 4000 (Central reservations).

Jersey European Airline: Flights from Exeter (Tel: 0392 64440) and Bournemouth (Tel: 0202 29255) to Dinard/St-Malo. Also Jersey (Tel: 0534 45661) to Dinard.

BANKS

Generally open between 9 and 12 and 2 and 5 weekdays, although most are shut all day Monday. All banks close Sundays and bank holidays. Always take your passport.

BUS SERVICES

Getting about by bus (*car* in French) in rural areas can be a problem as there is often only one bus a day, sometimes one bus a week, and they are frequently scheduled to tie in with market days or school starting and finishing times. Get a timetable from the local *Syndicat* or bus station.

CAR HIRE

Cars can be hired in most large towns but hiring is expensive mainly because of the large pencentage of VAT it incurs. Advance package deals are available through tour operators and Airline Companies in the form of fly-drive. French and British Railways also offer car rental in conjunction with rail travel. Also in the UK contact – Avis (081 848 8733), Budget (0800 181181), Godfrey Davis (081 950 5050), Hertz (081 679 1777).

CHILDREN

Don't be apprehensive about taking children to France. They will be made to feel welcome in bars, cafés and restaurants where you will not feel obliged to order a full meal for a small child. Airlines, ferry companies and the railways offer reduced rates for children and hotels usually have family rooms or will supply an extra bed or cot for a small additional charge. Supermarkets and chemists sell disposable nappies, milk powder and good-quality baby foods. In the major seaside resorts, the splendid clubs 'Mickey' can be found on the sands with supervisors overseeing the trampolines, slides, swings, climbing ropes and activities popular with children. Many tour operators offer free travel for children in the off-peak period.

COACH TRAVEL

National Express Eurolines operate a connecting system all

over the UK and Eire with through services to Paris (daily).
Personal bookings may be made at:

The Coach Centre, 13, Regent Street, London SW1.
Victoria Coach Station, Buckingham Palace Road, London
SW1.
Eurolines, 52, Grosvenor Gardens, London SW1.

Or book at any coach station or your local National Express
travel agent nationwide. You may also telephone their enquiry
centres:
London 071 730 0202, Manchester 061 228 3881, Birmingham
021 622 4373, Oxford 0865 791579, Cardiff 0222 44751,
Cambridge 0223 460711, Bristol 0272 541022, Leeds 0532
460011. Credit Card Reservations 071 730 8235.

A daily London/Paris coach service is also operated by
Hoverspeed, Maybrook House, Queens Gds., Dover CT17
9UQ. Tel: 0304 240241.

CREDIT CARDS

The major credit cards – American Express, Carte Bleue (Visa/
Barclaycard), Diners Club and Eurocard (Mastercard/Access)
– are widely accepted. Most offer free travel-accident
insurance.

CURRENCY

You may take unlimited amounts of currency into France but
if you are likely to be carrying a very large sum of money see
the notes in the section on Customs Formalities that follows.
It's always a good idea to get a small amount in francs from
your bank at home before leaving plus travellers cheques.
Enquire at your bank if they issue Eurocheques or something
similar, as these are extremely convenient and easy to use as

are Girocheques which can be cashed in French Post Offices. The French franc comes in both coin and banknote form. Notes are for 500, 200, 100, 50 and 20 francs. There are 100 centimes to the franc.

CUSTOMS FORMALITIES

Tax-free allowances change, so get a leaflet on board ship or at any air terminal for current allowances for tobacco, alcohol, perfume, etc. Cars, caravans, motorcycles, bicycles and boats, simply for the personal use of the tourist, are imported without formality but must be re-exported within six months. The same applies to personal effects which must not be used for commercial transactions or be sold. There is no limit to the amount of French and foreign banknotes you may bring into the country, but if you have more than the equivalent of 50,000 French francs it is advisable to declare this and complete a special customs form. This document will allow you, if necessary, to take back out of France an amount exceeding 50,000 francs, the maximum allowed.

DISABLED

In the case of less severely handicapped people, or those suffering from minor disabilities, individual tour operators will advise on types of holidays, amenities and services. For extremely handicapped people there are various organizations both in the UK and in France which can provide valuable information and help in making holiday arrangements. The larger airline companies all supply wheelchairs for use around their precincts and lifts for wheelchair access to aeroplanes. These should be arranged when booking. Registered blind people travelling by rail and Sealink to France can take a companion with them free of charge. A blind person's of Registration is required or a form from the Social Services. In France special facilities are available throughout the SNCF network. Ask for the free booklet listing these at any French mainline station (in French only). A special information sheet is also available from the French Government Tourist Office, 178 Piccadilly, London, W1V 0AL (enclose s.a.e. A4 size). A leaflet is also obtainable from Mobility International, 228 Borough High Street, London SE1. Tel: 071 403 5688; and a guide to holidays abroad which includes France is published annually by Radar, 25, Mortimer Street, London, W1. Tel: 071 637 5400. A series of 'Access' books, which not only provide general information but lists of hotels, etc. is published by Pauline Hephaistos Survey Projects, 39 Bradley Gds., West Ealing, London W13. Titles include *Access at the Channel Ports* and *Access in Brittany*. The books are free but postage and a donation are welcomed. Contact CNFLRH (Comité National Français de Liaison pour las Réadaptation des Handicapés), at 38 Boulevard Raspail, 75007 Paris, France, for their wheelchair guide to France: *Voyager Quand Même* (in French only but with English glossary and easily understood symbols), and for information on activity holidays for disabled people of all ages. It is also worth writing to the Loisirs Accueil in the area you have chosen to visit. See listings – TOURIST OFFICES and LOISIRS ACCUEIL.

DRIVING

Rules of the road are very similar to here apart from the main difference – drive on the right. Many people find the idea daunting but, with a little bit of extra concentration, it feels surprisingly natural after about fifteen minutes on the road. Danger points are when leaving a restaurant or garage when one's natural inclination is to pull away on the left. Caution should be exercised at junctions where in built-up areas *priorité à droite* (give way to the right) still applies. As in this country, priority is given to cars already on a roundabout. You have priority on all major roads and this is marked by the sign *passage protegé* or a tilted yellow square. Where a black bar crosses the square you no longer have priority. *Cédez le passage* also means Give Way. A G.B. sticker should be displayed at the rear of your vehicle and the following general rules should be observed:

Breakdown: You should carry a red warning triangle in case of breakdown and place it 30 metres behind the car to warn other drivers. In the case of an accident the police should be informed and a statement form completed.

Documents: Carry driving licence, certificate of insurance and car registration document or a letter authorizing you to drive it if the vehicle is not yours. A green card is not compulsory but will give you much better cover than your ordinary insurance which only gives minimum cover in France. Check with your insurance company, AA or RAC.
Breakdown insurance covers you for additional expenses such as hotel accommodation, hire car, towing, transporting costs, etc. should your vehicle be off the road for any length of time. Carry the breakdown insurance documents with you.
N.B. Driving on a provisional licence is not allowed. The minimum age to drive in France is eighteen.

Drinking/Driving: Police exercise random breath tests with very heavy penalties for exceeding the alcohol limit which is similar to here.

Lights: Full or dipped headlights should be used. Sidelights only when stationary. Beams should be adjusted for right-hand drive (adjusters can be bought in motoring shops here). Yellow discs are no longer compulsory in France but you must carry a spare bulb kit.

Seat Belts: Compulsory in the front. Children under ten must sit in the back.

Speeding: Heavy fines are imposed on the spot for exceeding the speed limits which are:

Toll motorways – 130 km per hour.

Dual carriageways and non toll motorways – 110 km per hour.

Other roads – 90 km per hour.

Towns/built up areas – 60 km per hour (except where signposted even lower).

N.B. In wet weather limits are reduced by 10 km per hour, 20 km on toll motorways.

Towing: On major roads and motorways leave a distance of at least fifty metres between yourself and the vehicle in front. A caravan or trailer must not exceed 2.5 metres in width and the vehicle should be fitted with good rear-view and side-view mirrors.

As France is such a large country it is still possible even in the height of summer to find secondary roads where the traffic is surprisingly light. If you are not travelling very long distances, or are not in a great hurry, these country roads are a much more pleasant way of getting from A to Z. Look out for the green arrow sign which indicates a route, often scenic, avoiding busy main roads. These routes, known as *Bison futé*, are shown on the special maps produced by the French Ministry of Transport and are available from the FGTO in London or can be picked up at Information Centres in France. However, France also has a good network of dual carriageways, motorways (*autoroutes*) and toll motorways (*autoroutes à péage*). Motorway signs are white on a blue background. Take a ticket as you enter the tollbooth. Keep it for the next toll check to calculate how much you have to pay. Payment is either directly into a machine, if you have the correct amount of change, or to the toll keeper. Credit cards are accepted as are sterling notes but the change will be in francs. In the event of a breakdown stay in the right-hand emergency lane with hazard lights on. Emergency telephones, orange in colour, are situated all along the motorways. Service areas are plentiful along the way, with restaurants, picnic areas, toilets, telephones, etc. All have facilities for disabled people.

Road classifications are –

A   (autoroute = Motorway)
N   (route nationale = Trunk road)
D   (route départementale = Secondary road)

COMMON SIGNS-
   arrêt autocars: Bus stop
   boue: Mud
   centre ville: Town centre
   chantier: Roadworks
   chaussée deformée: Uneven road surface
   déviation: Diversion
   gravillons: Loose chippings
   piste cyclable: Cycle path
   rappel: Remember (speed limit)
   route barrée: Road closed
   toutes directions: All directions
   autres directions: Other directions

EATING OUT

One of the most pleasurable experiences in France. Fairly rigid meal times – lunch starts at 12-12.30, dinner 7-7.30 with tables filling up rapidly. Sunday is the big 'eating out' day with restaurants full of family groups at lunchtime so get there early or pre-book.

ELECTRICITY

220 volts and 2-pin plugs are the norm. Take a continental adaptor with you.

FERRY COMPANIES

With five major cross-channel ferry companies offering large, modern ships with comfortable lounges, restaurants, cafeterias and duty-free shops, the crossing can be a pleasant part of your holiday.

It is advisable to book in advance, particularly for high season, at weekends, or if travelling with an overheight vehicle. Cabin accommodation, too, gets booked up very quickly. Check-in is normally one hour before departure (30 minutes for Hoverspeed).

The Crossings:–

Brittany Ferries, The Brittany Centre, Wharf Road, Portsmouth PO2 8RU. Tel: 0705 827701

Portsmouth/St Malo	9 hours day/10 hours night
Plymouth/Roscoff	6 hours day/7 hours night
Poole/Cherbourg	4½ hours day/5½ hours night
Portsmouth/Caen	5¾ hours day/6 hours night

(Arrives at the port of Ouistreham. Bus to Caen city centre about 45 minutes)

From Ireland

Cork/Roscoff	14 hours

Hoverspeed Ltd., Maybrook House, Queens Gardens, Dover. CT17 9UQ. Tel: 0304 240241

Dover/Calais	35 mins
Dover/Boulogne	40 mins

P & O European Ferries Ltd., Enterprise House, Channel
View Road, Dover. CT17 9TJ. Tel: 0304 203388

Dover/Calais	1¼ hours
Dover/Boulogne	1 hour 40 mins
Portsmouth/Cherbourg	4¾ hours day/6 hours night
Portsmouth/Le Havre	5¾ hours day/6½ hours night

From Ireland

Larne/Cairnryan	2¼ hours

Sally Line Ltd., 81 Piccadilly, London W1V 9HF. Tel: 071
409 2240.

Ramsgate/Dunkerque	2½ hours

Sealink U.K. Ltd., Charter House, Park Street, Ashford, Kent.
Tel: 0233 647033.

Dover/Calais	1½ hours
Folkestone/Boulogne	1 hour 50 mins
Newhaven/Dieppe	4 hours
Weymouth/Cherbourg	4 hours day/6 hours night
Portsmouth/Cherbourg	4¾ hours day/6 hours night

From Ireland –

Dun Laoghaire/Holyhead	3½ hours
Rosslare/Fishguard	3½ hours
Larne/Stranraer	2¼ hours
Dublin/Holyhead	3½ hours (B&I Line bookable through Sealink).

From the Channel Islands –

Commodore Shipping Services, 28 Conway Street, St Helier,
Jersey. Tel: 0534 71263.

Jersey/Saint Malo	1½ hours

Condor Hydrofoil, The North Pier Steps, St Peter Port,
Guernsey. Tel: 0481 26121.

Guernsey/Saint Malo	1¾ hours (foot passengers only)

Emeraude Ferries, 2, Albert Quay, St. Helier, Jersey. Tel: 0534
74458.

Jersey/Saint Malo   2½ hours

GARAGES

If not a self-service ask for *'le plein'* (fill her up) or a set amount, e.g., 200 francs. *'Super'* is top grade, *'essence'* for regular and *'sans plomb'* for unleaded. Diesel fuel is called *'gaz-oil'*.

Here too you can get the usual basic maintenance, checking tyres, oil and water levels, etc. Mechanical repairs are usually cheaper than in the UK although there can sometimes be a delay in getting parts for British cars. Most garages accept credit cards.

Useful phrases: *en panne*: broken down; *panne d'essence*: out of petrol; *pneu crevé*: flat tyre.
N.B. *pétrole* is French for paraffin!

HITCH-HIKING

The cheapest form of travel but illegal on motorways and, unlike other countries, at motorway services areas.
N.B. Young people under eighteen must carry a letter from their parents giving permission to hitch-hike.

INSURANCE (Holiday)

It is strongly advisable to take out holiday insurance against possible loss of money and baggage, medical expenses, accidents, delays and cancellation or curtailment of holiday. Shop around because amounts payable in compensation and exclusion clauses vary. When taking a car, the purchase of breakdown insurance is also advisable.

KILOS AND KILOMETRES/METRIC SYSTEM

1 kilo = 2.2 lb. 1 litre = 1¾ pints. 4½ litres = approx. 1 gallon.
1.6 kilometres = 1 mile. 1 metre = 39 inches.

A quick way to convert kilometres to miles – divide by 8 and
multiply by 5 – e.g. 8 kilometres = 5 miles.

To roughly convert Centigrade to Fahrenheit multiply by 2
and add 28.

MEDICAL

It is always advisable to take out private travel insurance for
the duration of your holiday to cover not only possible loss of
money and baggage but also medical expenses and hospital
costs. Before departure also apply to your local DHSS office or
main Post Office for the Form E111. If you are unfortunate
enough to fall ill on holiday you will have to pay the doctor on
the spot and the pharmacist who makes up your prescription.
Be sure to keep your receipts. Show the doctor your E111 form
and he will help you to fill in *une feuille de maladie*. After visiting
the chemist, attach the sticky labels from the bottles and boxes
to the *feuille de maladie* and then apply to the local French
Office of Social Security who will partially reimburse you
(around 70%), though not necessarily at the time. It is more
likely to be sent on to you.

PASSPORTS

A full British Passport or a British Visitor's Passport (forms
available at any main post office) is all that is required. For
non-British subjects, the French Consulate will advise on visas.
Remember to check before leaving that your passport is valid
until AFTER your planned return date.

POST

Post Offices (PTT) are normally open between 8 and 12, 2.30 and 7 and Saturday mornings. Mail can be sent to you c/o *Poste Restante* followed by the town and department number. Take your passport with you when collecting mail. In larger towns you can change money at Post Offices displaying a CHANGE sign. Letter-boxes are yellow and stamps can also be bought in *tabacs* (tobacco shops).

PUBLIC HOLIDAYS

The French tend to have rather more holidays than us, the main public holidays being:

New Year's Day	1st January
Labour Day	1st May
V.E. Day	8th May
Bastille Day	14th July
Assumption Day	15th August
All Saints Day	1st November
Armistice Day	11th November
Christmas Day	25th December

There are also holidays on Easter Monday, Ascension Day and Whit Monday. Dates vary from year to year.

RAIL TRAVEL

SNCF (French Railways) operate an excellent train service between Paris and numerous points in Brittany. For a quick arrival take the TGV high-speed train (*Train à Grande Vitesse*). Among the fastest in the world, it travels at up to 187mph, and extends into Brittany – to Brest via Rennes and La Baule via Nantes. Each train has a bar and buffet and meals are also served where you sit. For seeing the countryside, however, the slower 'all stations' kind of journey is best. Good restaurants and buffets are also to be found in stations, often even in the smallest. Certain trains – 'family trains' – have a special compartment for mothers and babies with nappy-changing tables, etc., and a play-room with games and toys for children. Arrangements can also be made for unaccompanied children to travel in the care of a railway hostess.

A *France Vacance* Pass – rail rover ticket, allows unlimited travel in France on any 4 days within 15 days or 9 or 16 days within a month. With a *Carte Jeune* under 26s qualify for up to 50 per cent reduction on rail travel. For Senior Citizens a *Carte Vermeil*, allowing similar reductions, may be purchased. There are, however, certain conditions relating to all of these and enquiries should be made well in advance. Car hire is available at many railway stations at reduced rates. Also bicycle hire.

N.B. Be sure to validate rail tickets bought in France at each stage of your journey by using the orange date-stamping machine (*composteur*) at the platform entrance. After an overnight stop you must date it again before rejoining the train. Failure to do this entails a surcharge of 20% of the fare with a fixed minimum charge. Paris is the focal point of the railway network. There are six main stations all of which are linked up with the Metro system and service different areas of the country – For Brittany: Paris Montparnasse.

Heavy luggage may be registered in advance and collected (or delivered) at your destination. Meals, seats and sleeping accommodation, may be booked in advance. For further information on all the above contact: French Railways, 179, Piccadilly, London W1V 0BA (personal callers) Tel: 071 409 3518 (Motorail only).
Or Intercity Europe/Eurotrain. Tel: 071 834 2345 (automatic call queuing). Or any British Rail Travel Centre, main-line station or travel agent.

SHOPPING

Pâtisseries to tempt you with a mouth-watering display of
superb pastries, *boulangeries* smelling of freshly baked bread,
markets piled high with fresh farm produce and freshly caught
fish – shopping in France is a delight. Food shops are usually
open from 8 in the morning till 7 or 8 in the evening with at
least a two-hour break in the middle of the day (the French
still enjoy a long leisurely lunch). This applies Mondays to
Saturdays but most open Sunday morning also. Many small
groceries are self-service (*supermarchés*) so there is no worry
about language problems. And then there are the
hypermarkets (*hypermarchés*), where you can buy anything from
a reel of cotton to a fridge-freezer and wheel the whole lot out
in a trolley (*chariot*) to your car in the giant car park. This is a
good place to buy your duty-free wine, choosing from the
many different varieties displayed on shelf after shelf. Other
good buys for last-minute shopping are – beer: very cheap and
there is a generous duty-free allowance; butter: very expensive
but delicious; cheese: an amazing variety; chocolate: cheap and
of good quality; coffee: almost half the UK price; jams:
delicious and with no additives; olive oils: sold in bargain-size
bottles; mustard: huge selection sold in attractive pots.

Other Shops

La blanchisserie – laundry. Useful to note here that laundrettes
    are almost non existent.
La charcuterie – delicatessen with wide choice of cooked meats,
    pâtés, regional specialities and salads. Also take-away dishes
    that can be cooked or re-heated at home.
Le coiffeur – hairdressers. Ask for '*un rendez-vous*' (an
    appointment). A cut is '*une coupe*'.
La droguerie – does not sell drugs as you might think but is like
    our old-fashioned hardware store. Pots and pans, corkscrews
    and tin-openers are piled high alongside soaps, shampoos

and insect sprays. Also items of camping equipment/
camping gas (*gaz*).

L'épicerie or *l'alimentation* – sells usual groceries plus wines, fruit,
vegetables and milk. (Red-topped bottles are full-cream
milk, blue-topped are semi-skimmed.) Beer, of the light
lager variety, can be bought here too, in packs of six or
twenty-four. Cheaper to buy in litre bottles which, like litre
wine and soft-drinks bottles, are subject to a small deposit.
Take the empties back for a refund to either the checkout
desk or in larger supermarkets the counter marked '*consignée*'
or '*reprise de bouteilles*'.

La maison de la presse – sells newspapers and magazines.

La parfumerie – as the name suggests, sells perfumes, also
cosmetics and beauty products. Can be pricey.

La pharmacie – chemist shop, but unlike the UK where you can
buy a variety of toiletries, mainly sells medicines. Easily
spotted by the large green cross outside.

La poissonnerie – fish shop. In coastal towns opening hours often
tie in with the catch.

Le pressing – dry cleaners.

Le tabac – the tobacconist. Stocks most British, French and
International brands. Also sells stamps.

SYNDICAT D'INITIATIVE/OFFICE DE TOURISME

Local Tourist Offices to be found in almost every town, large
or small. They are an invaluable source of information on
accommodation, local activities, museums, festivals, sightseeing,
bicycle hire, fishing permits, etc.

TAXIS

Taxi drivers charge a set pick-up fee plus so much per
kilometre. They can only pick you up from a taxi rank (*station*

de taxi) or by phone and should have a meter. Rates similar to the UK.

TELEPHONE

Within France the system is relatively easy to use and coin boxes are numerous. Calls made through hotel switchboards are likely to cost you more. All telephone numbers are eight figures and no extra dialling code is required when dialling from province to province or local calls within Paris. From Paris to the provinces the eight-figure number should be precded by 16. From the provinces to Paris dial 16 followed by 1 then the eight-figure number. To ring France from the UK dial 010 33 then the eight-figure number (provinces) or 010 33 1 then the eight-figure number (Paris).

To ring the UK from France dial 19, wait for the tone to change, dial 44 then the STD code (leaving off the 0) then the number.

You can receive calls at any phone booth, the telephone number is usually clearly displayed. Phone cards can be bought at Post Offices, or anywhere displaying the *Télécarte* sign, in 50 or 120 units.

Cheap rates – Monday to Friday: 9.30pm to 8am; Saturdays: After 2pm; Sundays and Public Holidays: All day.

Important numbers: Directory Enquiries: 12; Fire: 18; Operator: 13; Police: 17; Telegrams: 14.

TIME

One hour ahead of British time apart from October when it is the same.

TIPPING

The question of whether to tip or not has been greatly
simplified in recent years with the words *service compris* on the
bottom of most hotel and restaurant bills. It means service
included and it is not necessary to leave anything further.
Otherwise tipping is much the same as here (10-15%) and 2 or
3 francs to cinema and theatre attendants.

VOCABULARY

If you don't speak French take a good phrase book with you as
you will find that people are generally much more helpful if
you attempt at least a few words.

WATER

Safe to drink except where marked '*eau non potable*'. Large
selection of bottled waters on sale everywhere.

WEATHER

The weather in Northern Brittany is only marginally warmer
than the South of England. As you get into Southern Brittany
there's a considerable improvement with lots of long sunny
days between May and October. However, it can be wet, so do
pack a raincoat.

LISTINGS

ABBEYS, CHURCHES AND PARISH CLOSES

COTES-DU-NORD

Bulat-Pestivien
Notre-Dame-de-Bulat Church:
15th to 16th-century church with a 66m high spire added in the 19th century. Many interesting features include ancient carvings and statues. Three sacred fountains. *Pardon* in early September.

Châtelaudren
Notre-Dame-du-Tertre Church
15th-century church with an unusual series of 96 painted panels on the roof of the chancel. While these depict Biblical scenes a further 32 in a side chapel illustrate scenes from the lives of St Fiacre and St Margaret. *Pardon* during August.

Dinan
Lehon Abbey:
Founded in the 9th and rebuilt in the 13th century. 14th-century refectory, 17th-century cloister and some of the oldest stained glass to be found in Brittany.

Guingamp
Notre-Dame-de-Bon-Secours:
14th to 16th-century Basilica. One of Brittany's finest churches housing a Madonna carved in black stone. *Pardon* and candlelit procession in early July.

Kergrist-Moëlou
Notre-Dame Church:
Dates from the 16th century. Restored in the 19th. Marvellous sculptures along the south façade. Large ornate calvary in the grounds.

Kérity-Paimpol
Beauport Abbey:
Magnificent ruins of 13th-century church and refectory, four rooms perfectly preserved. 14th-century cloisters, abbey church, chapter-house and cellars.

Kerpert
Coat Mallouen Abbey:
Founded by the Cistercians in the 12th century. (Ruins).

Lannion
Brélévenez Church:
Dating from 12th century. 142 granite steps lead up to its Romanesque doorway. 15th-century bell tower. Fine paintings and altarpieces.

Lantic
Notre-Dame-de-la-Cour:
15th-century chapel. Stone vaults. Magnificent windows.

Perros-Guirec
Notre-Dame-de-la-Clarté:
Delightful 15th-century chapel in rose pink granite. The name stems from a local belief that the Virgin can restore clarity of sight. A procession of pilgrims is held in August each year.

Plenée-Jugon
Boquen Abbey:
12th-century abbey recently restored and now a convent.

Ploubezré
Kerfons Chapel:
Interior features include Renaissance rood screen and stained-glass windows. Ancient calvary in the grounds.

Plouha
Kermaria an Isquit Chapel:

13th-century Seigniorial chapel. Originally a courthouse and chapel; sentences were read from the exterior balcony. Famous '*Dance Macabre*' fresco depicting dancing skeletons.

Ploumilliau
Saint-Milliau Chapel:
17th-century chapel famous for its stone-carved Breton figure of death.

Runan
Notre-Dame-de-Runan Church:
Ornate 14th to 15th-century church with remarkable furnishings, sculptures, carved beams, columns and panels. Enormous 15th-century stained-glass window. The exterior is decorated with elaborately carved stone figures and coats of arms. Set in a parish close with calvary, its ossuary is dated 1552. Torchlit procession in July.

Saint-Brieuc
Saint-Etienne Cathedral:
Fortified cathedral dating from the 13th century in the old quarter of the town. Ancient tombs, carved wood altar, 15th-century windows and statues.

Saint-Gelven
Bon Repos Abbey:
12th-century Cistercian abbey built on the banks of the Blavet river in an attractive setting.

Saint-Nicolas-du-Pélem
Notre-Dame-du-Ruellou Chapel:
18th-century chapel with wooden carillon wheel of the same period with a dozen small bells.

Tréguier
Saint-Tugdual Cathedral:
Superb 13th to 15th-century building with unusual tall stone spire. Remarkable cloister with fine recumbent figures.

Famous festival each May when lawyers and advocates from all over France walk in procession from the cathedral.

Saint-Gonéry Chapel:
15th-century chapel with unusual spire. Biblical scenes painted on roof of nave.

FINISTERE

Briec
Saint-Vennec Chapel:
Gothic chapel containing many 15th and 16th-century sculptures and carvings. Remarkable group of Ste-Gwenn and her triplets. The saint had an additional breast enabling her to feed her three sons simultaneously.

Carhaix
Notre-Dame-du-Crann Chapel:
Beautifully preserved 16th-century chapel – original furnishings and stained glass.

Confort-Meilars
Notre-Dame-de-Confort Church:
16th-century church. Ancient stained-glass windows. In the nave is a carillon wheel with twelve bells which in former times were rung in the hope of curing speech defects.

Daoulas
Daoulas Abbey:
12th-century abbey church. Cloisters rebuilt but nevertheless a good example of Romanesque architecture.

Le Folgoët
Basilica of Notre-Dame:
15th-century church with fine porch. Many examples of ancient Breton art include carved granite rood screen, five altars, statues and stained-glass windows. Outside against the apse wall is a sacred fountain where pilgrims come to drink.

Famous as a pilgrimage centre, a great *pardon* (one of the largest in Brittany) takes place in early September.

Landevennec
Saint-Guénolé Abbey:
Benedictine abbey founded in the 5th century (ruins). New abbey built in 1958 nearby.

Locmaria
Notre-Dame Church:
Romanesque church with 11th-century nave. 12th-century transepts.

Locronan
Saint-Ronan Church:
15th-16th century. Tomb and statue of the Irish monk Saint Ronan. 16th to 17th-century carvings, decoration and stained-glass window. Ornate cross in the cemetery.
Notre-Dame-de-Bonne-Nouvelle:
Attractive 16th-century chapel. Typical Breton setting with calvary and fountain.

Loctudy
Saint-Tudy Church:
18th-century façade. 12th-century Romanesque interior – the best preserved in Brittany. Unusual animal and human carvings.

Plounéour-Ménez
Relecq Abbey:
Ruins of 12th-century Cistercian church.

Quimper
Saint-Corentin Cathedral:
One of the finest examples of a Gothic cathedral in Brittany dating mainly from the 13th century set in the medieval quarter of Quimper. 13th-century chancel, and 15th-century transept, nave and stained-glass. The twin spires were added in 1856.

Quimperlé
Sainte-Croix Church:
12th-17th century. Modelled on the design of the Church of
the Holy Sepulchre in Jerusalem – a rotunda with three little
bays and a porch making a Greek cross. Fine Renaissance
screen and altarpiece. Crypt.

Rumengol
Notre-Dame-des-Guérisons:
15th to 17th-century church with ancient statue of Our Lady.
Nearby sacred fountain. *Pardons* on Trinity Sunday and
Assumption day dedicated to Our Lady of All Remedies.

Saint-Herbot
Saint-Herbot Chapel:Gothic chapel named after the patron saint
of horned animals. In front of the church a 16th-century
sculpture depicting the saint and his animals.

Saint-Pol-de-Léon
Saint-Pol—Aurélian Cathedral:
13th to 16th-century church (formerly a cathedral). Elegant
Gothic building with tall twin towers. Carved 16th-century
choir stalls, and altar decorations. Renaissance stained glass
windows. Tombs and relics.
Notre-Dame-du-Kreisker Church:
14th to 15th-century towering over the nearby cathedral.
Superb bell tower, 77m high. Climb the tower for panoramic
views.

Trémalo
Trémalo Chapel:
Breton chapel containing the 16th-century wooden figure of
Christ used as the model for Gauguin's 'Yellow Christ''.

ILLE ET VILAINE

Bais
Saint-Mars Church:

16th to 19th century. Large gabled porch originally built for
the local lepers who were not allowed into the church.
Intricately carved doorway.

Champeaux
Sainte-Barbe Church:
15th century. Many examples of 16th-century art. Beautifully
carved oak choir-stalls and stained-glass window.

Dol-de-Bretagne
Saint-Samson Cathedral:
13th century. Twin towered vast cathedral. Large south
porch added in 14th and 15th century. Eighty 14th-century
choir-stalls exquisitely carved.

Les Iffs
Des Iffs Church:
Takes its name from the yew trees in its churchyard. Superb
14th to 15th-century Breton church. Renowned for its nine
windows of 16th-century Breton glass showing Biblical scenes.
Large porch originally built to allow lepers to celebrate mass.

Fougères
Saint-Sulpice Church:
Mainly 15th century with unusually tall and graceful spire.
Louis XV wood carvings and a 12th-century statue of the
Virgin believed to work miracles.

Langon
Saint-Pierre Church
12th century. Unusual tower encircled by twelve small
towers.

Redon
Saint-Sauveur Basilica:
12th to 17th-century Romanesque abbey church. 13th-
century fresco and chancel. Nave roofed with a Romanesque
wooden vault. Nearby stands a separate 13th-century Gothic
tower. 57m high, cut off from the church by fire in 1780.

Rennes

Saint-Pierre Cathedral:

18th century. 16th-century altarpiece depicting scenes from the Virgin's life. Gilded columns.

Saint-Germain Church:

16th century in Flamboyant Gothic style. Superb east window. 18th-century gilded canopy above the altar.

Saint-Malo

Saint-Vincent Cathedral:

Restored Gothic cathedral. 12th-century nave. 13th-century chancel. Beautiful modern stained-glass windows.

MORBIHAN

Auray

Saint-Avoye Chapel:

16th-century chapel with beautifully carved rood screen.

La Faouët

Saint-Fiacre Chapel:

15th-century chapel famous for its carved and painted rood screens.

Sainte-Barbe Chapel:

Small chapel in a pretty setting overlooking the Valley of the Elle. Dates from 1500. Renaissance stained-glass, carvings and statues. Outside a bell rung by pilgrims in the hope of having their prayers answered. *Pardons* in June and December.

Kernascléden

Notre-Dame-de-Kernascléden

15th-century Gothic chapel. 15th-century Renaissance frescoes of Biblical scenes and remarkable 'Dance of Death' showing the torturing of the damned.

Langonnet

Notre-Dame Abbey:

12th-century Cistercian monastery restored in the 17th and 18th centuries.

Pluméliau

Saint-Nicodème Chapel:

Renaissance chapel with bell tower and tall spire which can be climbed. 16th-century doorway. Numerous statues. Gothic fountain outside. *Pardon* in August.

Sainte-Anne-d'Auray

Sainte-Anne d'Auray Church:

Part of an important religious centre. Vast 19th-century church built on the site of the original 17th-century chapel. Walls decorated with pilgrims' offerings, some dating back three hundred years. *Pardons* throughout the year including the famous one on 25th and 26th July.

Saint-Ave

Notre-Dame-du-Loc Chapel:

15th-century chapel with interesting wooden carvings and wooden calvary. Altar statues dating from the 15th century.

Vannes

Saint-Pierre Cathedral:

Set in the old town. Dates from 13th century. Romanesque bell tower. 16th-century round tower containing relics of a Spanish missionary. Fine 17th-century tapestries.

PARISH CLOSES

The *enclos paroissial* (parish close) is a unique feature of Brittany though mainly located in Finistère. The parish church is enclosed by a wall with a triumphal arch, and within its precincts are a calvary, often with numerous elaborately sculptured figures, an ossuary (for storing the bones of the dead), and sometimes a fountain and graveyard. Built mainly in the 16th and 17th centuries they represent an important aspect of the Breton cultural heritage and religious

life. The most interesting and elaborate are to be found in
Finistère at:

    Argol
    Brasparts
    Guimiliau
    Lampoul-Guimiliau
    La Martyre
    Pleyben
    Saint-Thégonnec
    Sizun

AQUARIA, BIRD SANCTUARIES, PARKS AND ZOOS

(Consult local Tourist Offices for days and times)

COTES-DU-NORD

Cap-Fréhel
Bird sanctuary on spectacular headland north of Dinan.
Sept-Iles
Boat trips from Perros-Guirec to Sept-Iles bird sanctuary.
Permanent exhibition at Ile-Grande bird sanctuary.
Trégomeur
Wild life park and zoo.

FINISTERE

Audierne
Les Grands Viviers Aquarium.
Cap Sizun
Bird sanctuary on wild cliffs near Pointe du Raz.
Landerneau
Saint-Urbain Zoo.
Plogastel-Saint-Germain
De la Pommeraie Zoo.
Roscoff

Charles Pérez Zoo.
Sizun
Aquarium.

ILLE ET VILAINE

Betton
Ouestland - The Park of Brittany. Large modern theme park
with lots of amusements.
Dinard
Sea Aquarium and Museum.
Fougères
Chénedet Recreation Centre. Hiking, cycling and boating.
Iffendic
In Trémelin Park. Leisure centre with lake, mini-golf, cycling
and riding.
Lanhelin
Cobac-Park. Recreation centre. Riding, fishing, shooting,
dancing, barbecues, miniature railway.
Pléchatel
Tertre-Gris Park. Recreation park near Bain-de-Bretagne for
hiking, canoeing and picnicking.
Pleugueneuc
La Bourbansais Castle Zoo.
Rennes-Cesson-Sévigné
Aquarium.
Saint-Malo
Aquarium.

MORBIHAN

Le Guerno
Branféré Park.
Langonnet
Le Hoslay Zoo.
Pont-Scorff
Kerruisseau Park.

Quiberon
Aquarium.
Vannes
Aquarium.

BICYCLE HIRE AT RAILWAY STATIONS

Stations in the following towns hire out bicycles —
Auray (Morbihan)
La Baule (Loire-Atlantique)
Brest (Finistère)
Châteaulin (Finistère)
Combourg (Ille-et-Vilaine)
Concarneau (Finistère)
Le Croisic (Loire-Atlantique)
Dinan (Côtes-du-Nord)
Dinard (Ille-et-Vilaine)
Dol-de-Bretagne (Ille-et-Vilaine)
Douarnenez/Tréboul (Finistère)
Guingamp (Côtes-du-Nord)
Lamballe (Côtes-du-Nord)
Lannion (Côtes-du-Nord)
Lorient (Morbihan)
Morlaix (Finistère)
Pornic (Lorie-Atlantique)
Pornichet (Loire-Atlantique)
Quiberon (Morbihan)
Quimper (Finistère)
Rennes (Ille-et-Vilaine)
Roscoff (Finistère)
Saint-Brieuc (Côtes-du-Nord)
Saint-Malo (Ille-et-Vilaine)
Saint-Sébastien (Finistère)
Vannes (Morbihan)

N.B. Although Loire-Atlantique is no longer officially part of Brittany, some stations in this area have been included.

BOAT TRIPS

(For days and times contact local Tourist Offices)

BOAT TRIPS TO THE ISLANDS

COTES-DU-NORD

To Ile de Bréhat
From Paimpol (Pointe de l'Arcouest).
From Erquy.
From Perros-Guirec (Plage de Trestraou).

To Les Sept Iles (Bird Sanctuary)
From Perros-Guirec (Plage de Trestraou).

FINISTERE

To Ile de Batz
From Roscoff.

To Iles de Glénan
From Bénodet, Quimper and Loctudy.
From Beg-Meil and Port-la-Forêt.
From Concarneau.
To Ile d'Ouessant and Ile de Molène
From Brest (Port de Commerce)
To Ile de Sein
From Audierne.

ILLE-ET-VILAINE

To Iles de Chausey

From Saint-Malo (Gare Maritime de la Bourse).
From Dinard.

MORBIHAN

To Ile aux Moines
From Port-Blanc.
To Belle-Ile
From Quiberon.
From Vannes (Le Pont-Vert).
From La Trinité-sur-Mer (Cours-des-Quais).
To Ile de Groix
From Lorient (Quai de l'Estacade).
To Ile d'Houat and Ile d'Hoëdic
From Quiberon
From Vannes (Gare Maritime).

BOAT TRIPS ON SEA, RIVERS AND WATERWAYS.

COTES-DU-NORD

Trieux Estuary
3 hour trip from Pointe de l'Arcouest along the estuary to La Roche-Jagu castle.
Dinan/Rance Valley
River trip along the Rance to Dinard and back by coach. Two-and-a-half hours.
Pink Granite Coast
Sea trips along the coast from Plage de Trestraou, Perros-Guirec to Ploumanac'h.
Guerlédan Lake
Trips on Guerlédan lake located about 10 miles from Pontivy.

FINISTERE

Odet Estuary
River trips along the Odet river as far as Quimper from Bénodet, Loctudy, Beg-Meil, Port-la-Forêt, Concarneau and Sainte-Marine.
Aulne River
River trips up the Aulne river from Châteauneuf-du-Faou.
Concarneau/Beg-Meil
Regular sea trips across the bay between these two towns. Duration 30 minutes.
Camaret-sur-Mer
Sea trips from Camaret to Pointe de Penhir and Les Tas de Pois. Approx. one-and-a-half-hours.
Douarnenez
Trips around the bay of Douarnanez to Morgat.
Crozon Peninsula
Sea trips from Crozon-Morgat.
Brest
Trips around the bay starting from the Port de Commerce, Brest.
Roscoff
Three-hour sea trips around Morlaix Bay.
Le Conquet
Sea trips north to Pointe de Corsen, duration one-and-half hours, and south to Saint-Mathieu, duration one hour.

ILLE-ET-VILAINE

Le Vivier-sur-Mer
Sea trips around the bay of Le Mont-St-Michel.
Vilaine River
River trips along the Vilaine starting from Rennes.
Ille-et-Rance Canal
Canal trips from Rennes.
Saint-Malo/Dinard

River trips along the estuary of the Rance from Saint-Malo and Dinard as far as Dinan.

MORBIHAN

Gulf of Morbihan
Sea trips from Vannes, Port-Navalo, Arzon, Auray, Locmariaquer and Ile Aux Moines.
Etel River
Trips along the river starting from Etel.
Lorient
Trips round the bay, along the Blavet river and to the citadel of Port-Louis from Lorient.
Auray River
River trips starting from Port de Saint-Goustan, Auray.
Vilaine River
River trips along the Vilaine from Arzal to La Roche-Bernard and Redon.

CAMPSITES

Apply direct for current rates. Address should read as follows: name of the site, then town, then Department no. (Sites are not listed in Departments, however, the first two digits of the place number indicate its location: 22 = Côtes-du-Nord; 29 = Finistère; 35 = Ille-et-Vilaine; 56 = Morbihan.

Ambon 56190
   *** *Relais de l'Ocean*. Open 15/6 – 15/9. 90 places.
   Tel: 97 41 66 48.
Arradon 56610
   *** *Pen Boch*. Open 1/5 – 20/9. 125 places. Pool.
   Tel: 97 44 71 29.
Arzon 56640
   ** *Bilouris*. Open all year. 100 places. Tel: 97 53 70 56.
Audierne 29770

** *Kerhuon*. Open 1/4 – 30/9. 50 places. Tel: 98 70 10 91.

Auray 56400

** *Les Pommiers (Branhoc)*. Open all year. 150 places. Pool.
Tel: 97 24 01 48.

Baden 56870

*** *Mane Guernehue*. Open 1/4 – 15/10. 90 places. Pool.
Tel: 97 57 02 06.

Baguer-Pican 35120

**** *Du Vieux Chêne*. Open Easter – 30/9. 100 places. Pool.
Tel: 99 48 09 55.

Bain-de-Bretagne 35470

** *Municipal le Lac*. Open 1/4 – 31/10. 120 places.
Tel: 99 43 85 67.

Baud 56150

*** *Pont Augan*. Open 15/6 – 15/9. 32 places.
Tel: 97 51 04 74.

La Baule 44500

**** *La Roseraie*. Open Easter – 30/9. 120 places. Pool.
Tel: 40 60 46 66.

*** *Municipal*. Open 24/3 – 30/9. 350 places.
Tel: 40 60 11 48.

*** *Les Ajoncs d'Or*. Open Easter – 15/10. 200 places. Pool.
Tel: 40 60 33 29.

Beg-Meil 29170

*** *La Piscine*. Open 1/4 – 30/9. 92 places. Pool.
Tel: 98 56 56 06.

*** *La Roche Percée*. Open 15/5 – 30/9. 150 places. Pool.
Tel: 98 94 94 15.

*** *Le Vorlen*. Open 20/5 – 20/9. 600 places. Pool.
Tel: 98 94 97 36.

** *Kerolland*. Open 15/5 – 30/9. 165 places.
Tel: 98 94 91 00.

Belle-Ile-en-Mer 56360

*** *Bordénéo (Le Palais)*. Open 1/6 – 20/9. 165 places.
Tel: 97 31 88 96.

** *Municipal de Lannivrec (Locmaria)*. Open 1/6 – 15/9. 135 places. Tel: 97 31 73 75.

Belle-Isle-en-Terre 22810

** *Municipal les Forges*. Open 15/6 – 15/9. 200 places.
Tel: 96 43 30 38.

Bénodet 29950

**** *Letty*. Open 21/6 – 6/9. 511 places. Tel: 98 57 04 69.

**** *Pointe St Gilles*. Open 1/5 – 30/9. 485 places. Pool.
Tel: 98 57 05 37.

*** *Port de Plaisance*. Open 15/5 – 30/9. 242 places. Pool.
Tel: 98 57 02 38.

** *La Plage*. Open 1/6 – 15/9. 300 places. Pool.
Tel: 98 57 00 55.

** *Polquer*. Open 1/6 – 30/9. 250 places. Pool.
Tel: 98 57 04 19.

Binic 22520

**** *Le Panoramic*. Open 20/3 – 30/9. 180 places.
Tel: 96 73 60 43.

Brehat 22870

** *Municipal Goareva*. Open 15/6 – 15/9. 100 places.
Tel: 96 20 00 36.

Brignogan-Plages 29890

** *Du Phare*. Open 13/5 – 30/9. 150 places.
Tel: 98 83 45 67.

Camaret-sur-Mer 29570

*** *Trez Rouz*. Open Easter – 30/9. 78 places.
Tel: 98 27 93 96.

*** *Lambezen*. Open Easter – 30/9. 85 places. Pool.
Tel: 98 27 91 41.

Cancale 35260

*** *Le Bel Air*. Open Easter – 30/9. 280 places. Pool.
Tel: 99 89 64 36.

*** *Notre-Dame du Verger*. Open 25/3 – 30/9. 67 places.
Tel: 99 89 72 84.

*** *Port-Mer*. Open Easter – 30/9. 85 places.
Tel: 99 89 63 17.

** *Municipal Grouin*. Open 7/3 – 30/9. 166 places.
Tel: 99 89 63 79.

Carantec 29660

**** *Les Mouettes*. Open Easter – 30/9. 150 places. Pool.
Tel: 98 67 02 46.

Carnac 56340

**** *La Grande Métairie*. Open 27/5 – 16/9. 352 places.
Pool. Tel: 97 52 24 01.

**** *Les Menhirs*. Open 1/5 – 1/10. 250 places. Pool.
Tel: 97 52 94 67.

**** *Rosnual*. Open 1/5 – 30/9. 160 places. Pool.
Tel: 97 52 14 57.

*** *L'Étang*. Open 1/4 – 31/10. 165 places. Pool.
Tel: 97 52 14 06.

*** *Le Moulin de Kermeaux*. Open Easter – 16/9. 120 places.
Pool. Tel: 97 52 15 90.

*** *Les Pins*. Open all year. 160 places. Pool.
Tel: 97 52 18 90.

*** *Les Saules*. Open Easter – 30/9. 80 places. Pool.
Tel: 97 52 14 98.

*** *Moustoir*. Open 1/6 – 10/9. 165 places. Pool.
Tel: 97 52 16 18.

Caurel 22530

**** *Nautic International*. Open 1/4 – 15/10. 80 places. Pool.
Tel: 96 28 57 94.

La Chapelle-aux-Filtzméens 35190

**** *Du Château*. Open 15/5 – 15/9. 199 places. Pool.
Tel: 99 45 21 55.

Châteaugiron 35410

** *Municipal Les Grands Bosquets*. Open 1/4 – 30/9. 33
places. Tel: 99 37 41 69.

Châteauneuf-du-Faou 29520

*** *Municipal Penn Ar Pont*. Open 25/3 – 30/9. 120 places.
Pool. Tel: 98 81 81 25.

Combourg 35270

** *Municipal Le Vieux Chatel*. Open 1/6 – 31/8. 73 places.

Tel: 99 73 07 03.

Commana 29450

** *Municipal du Brennec*. Open 1/7 – 31/8. 50 places.

Tel: 98 78 00 13.

Concarneau 29900

*** *Les Prés Verts*. Open 15/6 – 15/9. 150 places.

Tel: 98 97 09 74.

** *Kerseaux*. Open 15/6 – 10/9. 200 places.

Tel: 98 97 37 41.

** *Lanadan*. Open 15/6 – 15/9. 110 places.

Tel: 98 97 17 78.

** *Lochrist*. Open all year. 100 places. Tel: 98 97 25 95.

Le Conquet 29217

** *Municipal le Theven*. Open Easter – 15/10. 450 places.

Tel: 98 89 06 90.

Crach 56950

*** *Le Fort Espagnol*. Open 29/5 – 16/9. 170 places. Pool.

Tel: 97 55 14 88.

Crozon 29160

*** *La Plage de Goulien*. Open 5/6 – 20/9. 90 places.

Tel: 98 27 17 10.

*** *Les Pins*. Open 5/6 – 20/9. 120 places.

Tel: 98 27 21 95.

*** *Pen Ar Menez*. Open Easter – 30/9. 200 places.

Tel: 98 27 12 36.

Damgan 56750

*** *Municipal le Mar*. Open 1/5 – 30/9. 100 places.

Tel: 97 41 02 31.

** *La Côte d'Amour*. Open Easter – 30/9. 100 places.

Tel: 97 41 11 39.

** *Le Roden*. Open Easter – 30/9. 130 places.

Tel: 97 41 16 70.

** *Oasis Camping*. Open 1/5 – 30/9. 150 places.

Tel: 97 41 10 52.

Dinan 22100

** *Municipal Châteaubriand*. Open 15/4 – 31/10. 50 places.

Tel: 96 39 11 96.

Dinard 35800

**** *Le Prieuré*. Open 20/3 – 1/10. 100 places.

Tel: 99 46 20 04.

*** *Municipal Port Blanc*. Open 1/4 – 30/9. 500 places.

Tel: 99 46 10 74.

Dol-de-Bretagne 35120

**** *Castel Camping des Ormes (Epiniac)*. Open 20/5 – 10/9.
400 places. Pool. Tel: 99 48 10 19.

** *Municipal les Tendières*. Open 1/5 – 30/9. 95 places.

Tel: 99 48 14 68.

Douarnenez/Tréboul 29100

** *Croas Men*. Open Easter – 30/9. 80 places.

Tel: 98 74 00 18.

** *Municipal le Bois d'Isis*. Open 15/6 – 15/9. 150 places.

Tel: 98 74 05 67.

** *Ferme de Kerleyou*. Open 30/4 – 15/9. 100 places.

Tel: 98 74 03 52.

** *Trézulien*. Open Easter – 15/9. 200 places.

Tel: 98 74 12 30.

Erdeven 56410

**** *Airotel Kerzerho*. Open Easter – 30/9. 250 places. Pool.

Tel: 97 55 63 17.

*** *Ideal Camping*. Open Easter – 15/9. 35 places.

Tel: 97 55 67 66.

*** *Les Sept Saints*. Open 1/5 – 15/9. 200 places. Pool.

Tel: 97 55 52 65.

Erquy 22430

*** La Plage St-Pabu. Open Easter – 30/9. 350 places.

Tel: 96 72 24 65.

*** *Le Vieux Moulin*. Open 1/4 – 15/9. 170 places. Pool.

Tel: 96 72 34 23.

*** *Bellevue*. Open Easter – 30/9. 100 places. Pool.

Tel: 96 72 33 04.

*** *Les Pins*. Open 15/5 – 15/9. 300 places. Pool.

Tel: 96 72 31 12.

Etables-sur-Mer 22680

   *** *L'Abri Côtier*. Open 1/4 – 30/9. 140 places.

   Tel: 96 70 61 57.

Le Faouët 56320

   *** *Municipal Beg Er Roc*. Open 1/3 – 15/9. 100 places.

   Tel: 97 23 15 11.

La Forêt-Fouesnant 29940

   **** *Le Manoir de Pen Ar Stir*. Open all year. 105 places.

   Tel: 98 56 97 75.

   **** *St Laurent*. Open 1/4 – 15/9. 300 places. Pool.

   Tel: 98 56 97 65.

   ** *La Plage*. Open 1/5 – 30/9. 80 places. Tel: 98 56 96 25.

   ** *Kerleven*. Open 15/6 – 30/9. 150 places.

   Tel: 98 56 98 83.

   ** *Kersioual*. Open 1/6 – 15/9. 180 places.

   Tel: 98 56 96 39.

   ** *Les Saules*. Open 15/6 – 15/9. 110 places.

   Tel: 98 56 98 57.

Fouesnant 29170

   ** *La Grande Allée*. Open Easter – 30/9. 120 places.

   Tel: 98 56 52 95.

   ** *Les Mimosas (Cap-Coz)*. Open 15/6 – 15/9. 80 places.

   Tel: 98 56 55 81.

   ** *Penan Cap*. Open 15/6 – 15/9. 100 places.

   Tel: 98 56 09 23.

   ** *La Plage (Cap-Coz)*. Open 15/6 – 15/9. 170 places.

   Tel: 98 56 00 59.

Fougères 35300

   *** *Municipal Paron*. Open all year. 90 places.

   Tel: 99 99 40 81.

La Gacilly 56200

   *** *Municipal le Bout du Pont*. Open 1/6 – 30/9. 94 places.

   Tel: 99 08 15 28.

Groix 56590

   *** *Les Sables Rouges*. Open 3/6 – 10/9. 125 places.

   Tel: 97 86 81 32.

Guidel 56520
   *** *Kergal*. Open 1/4 – 30/9. 132 places. Tel: 97 05 98 18.
Le Guilvinec 29730
   *** *La Plage*. Open 1/4 – 30/9. 410 places. Pool.
   Tel: 98 58 61 90.
Le Huelgoat 29690
   ** *Municipal du Lac*. Open 15/6 – 15/9. 100 places. Pool.
   Tel: 98 99 78 80.
Ile-d'Arz 56840
   ** *Municipal les Tamaris*. Open 1/6 – 30/9. 70 places.
   Tel: 97 44 30 35.
Ile-Tudy 29980
   ** *Municipal le Sillon*. Open Easter – 15/9. 178 places.
   Tel: 98 56 43 39.
   ** *Le Bois d'Amour*. Open 15/6 – 15/9. 74 places.
   Tel: 98 56 43 54.
Jugon-les-Lacs 22270
   ** *Municipal le Bocage*. Open 1/5 – 30/9. 240 places. Pool.
   Tel: 96 31 60 16.
Lamballe 22400
   ** *Municipal St Sauveur*. Open 15/6 – 15/9. 35 places.
   Tel: 96 31 00 61.
Lampaul-Ploudalmézeau 29830
   ** *Municipal les Dunes*. Open 15/6 – 15/9. 76 places.
   Tel: 98 48 09 84.
Lancieux 22770
   ** *Le Villeu*. Open 1/5 – 15/9. 200 places.
   Tel: 96 86 21 67.
   ** *Municipal les Mielles*. Open 1/4 – 30/9. 200 places.
   Tel: 96 86 22 98.
Landerneau 29800
   ** *Municipal*. Open 15/5 – 15/10. 40 places.
   Tel: 98 21 66 59.
Landudec 29710
   *** *Bel Air*. Open 15/6 – 15/9. 140 places. Pool.
   Tel: 98 91 50 27.

Lannion 22300
  *** *Beg Léguer*. Open 1/5 – 30/9. 200 places.
  Tel: 96 47 25 00.
Larmor-Baden 56790
  ** *Ker Eden*. Open 15/6 – 15/9. 100 places.
  Tel: 97 57 05 23.
Lesconil 29740
  *** *Des Dunes*. Open Easter – 30/9. 90 places.
  Tel: 98 87 81 78.
  *** *La Grande Plage*. Open 1/4 – 30/9. 80 places.
  Tel: 98 87 83 64.
  ** *Les Sables Blancs*. Open 1/6 – 15/9. 100 places.
  Tel: 98 87 84 79.
Locmariaquer 56740
  ** *Lann Brick*. Open 1/6 – 15/9. 100 places.
  Tel: 97 57 32 79.
Locquirec 29241
  ** *Municipal Les Pins-Toul Ar Goue*. Open 1/5 – 15/9. 200
  places. Tel: 98 67 40 85.
Locronan 29180
  ** *Municipal*. Open 1/6 – 30/9. 155 places.
  Tel: 98 91 87 76.
Loctudy 29750
  ** *Kergall*. Open Easter – 30/9. 100 places.
  Tel: 98 87 45 93.
  ** *Les Hortensias*. Open 1/7 – 31/8. 100 places.
  Tel: 98 87 46 64.
Locunole 29310
  **** *Le Ty Nadan*. Open 1/2 – 15/9. 200 places. Pool.
  Tel: 98 71 75 47.
Louannec 22700
  *** *Municipal Ernest Renan*. Open 15/6 – 15/9. 200 places.
  Tel: 96 23 11 78.
Louargat 22540
  **** *Manoir du Cleuziou*. Open 1/4 – 30/11. 200 places.
  Pool. Tel: 96 43 14 90.

Loudéac 22600
   ** *Municipal Les Ponts Es Bigot*. Open 15/6 – 15/9. 75
   places.
   Tel: 96 28 14 92.

Moëlan-sur-Mer 29350
   *** *La Grande Lande*. Open Easter – 30/9. 100 places.
   Tel: 98 39 71 92.

Mousterlin 29170
   **** *L'Atlantique*. Open 1/4 – 30/10. 150 places. Pool.
   Tel: 98 56 14 44.
   *** *Le Grand Large*. Open 15/6 – 15/9. 300 places.
   Tel: 98 56 04 06.
   ** *Cleut Rouz*. Open 1/4 – 30/9. 100 places.
   Tel: 98 56 06 45.
   ** *Kost Ar Moor*. Open 1/4 – 30/9. 360 places.
   Tel: 98 56 04 16.

Mur-de-Bretagne 22530
   ** *Municipal Rond Point Du Lac*. Open 15/6 – 15/9. 133
   places. Tel: 96 26 01 90.

Névez 29920
   **** *Le Raguenez Plage*. Open Easter – 30/9. 287 places.
   Tel: 98 06 80 69.
   *** *Les Deux Fontaines*. Open 1/6 – 30/9. 240 places. Pool.
   Tel: 98 06 81 91.
   *** *Saint Nicolas*. Open 1/5 – 30/9. 175 places.
   Tel: 98 06 89 75.

Paimpol 22500
   ** *Municipal Cruckin Kerity*. Open Easter – 30/9. 200 places.
   Tel: 96 20 78 47.

Penestin 56760
   **** *Airotel Domaine d'Inly*. Open 15/4 – 15/9. 500 places.
   Pool. Tel: 99 90 35 09.
   **** *Les Iles*. Open 15/4 – 30/9. 115 places. Pool.
   Tel: 99 90 30 24.
   *** *Des Parcs*. Open 15/4 – 30/9. 65 places.
   Tel: 99 90 30 59.

above: Vannes Château
(Photo: Corbel CRTB)

right: Rochefort-en-Terre

left: Fête de Cornouaille, Quimper *(photo: Corbel CRTB)*

below: Standing stones at Carnac

right: La Trinite-sur-Mer, Morbihan *(Explorer: photo: P. Plisson)*

below right: Calvary at Guehenno *(French Government Tourist Office)*

right: Ille-et-Rance Canal
(*The Telegraph Colour Library*)

below: The wild Finistere coast (*Photo: Rainon*)

opposite right: St-Servan – Solidor tower on the right (*Explorer: photo: P. H. Roy*)

below right: Fête de Rennes (*French Government Tourist Office: photo: Ogier*)

left: A Breton weaver *(French Government Tourist Office)*

above: The rocks at Ploumanac'h *(Explorer: photo P. H. Roy)*

above left: Perros-Guirec *(French Government Tourist Office: photo Charaffi)*

opposite left: A street in Dinan

above: Port Coton, Belle Ile *(Explorer: photo S. Cordier)*

left: The coastline at La Garde *(Explorer: photo J. Giganovic)*

*** *L'Armor*. Open 15/6 – 15/9. 90 places.
Tel: 99 90 31 28.
*** *Le Cénic*. Open Easter – 30/9. 90 places. Pool.
Tel: 99 90 33 14.

Penmarc'h 29760
** *La Joie*. Open 1/4 – 30/10. 260 places.
Tel: 98 58 63 24.

Perros-Guirec 22700
**** *Le Ranolien*. Open 3/2 – 13/11. 450 places. Pool.
Tel: 96 91 43 58.
*** *La Claire Fontaine*. Open 15/6 – 15/9. 180 places.
Tel: 96 23 03 55.
*** *Trestraou*. Open Easter – 30/9. 180 places. Pool.
Tel: 96 23 08 11.

Plancoët 22130
** *Municipal le Verger*. Open 15/6 – 15/9. 100 places.
Tel: 96 84 03 42.

Plérin 22190
*** *Municipal le Surcouf*. Open Easter – 30/9. 138 places.
Tel: 96 73 06 22.

Plestin-les-Grèves 22310
*** *Kerallic*. Open 11/6 – 16/9. 60 places.
Tel: 96 35 61 49.

Pleubian 22610
*** *Port la Chaine*. Open 1/6 – 10/9. 200 places.
Tel: 96 22 92 38.

Pleumeur-Bodou 22560
*** *L'Abri Côtier (Ile Grande)*. Open 1/4 – 15/9. 135 places.
Tel: 96 91 92 03.

Pleyben 29190
** *Municipal Pont Coblant*. Open 15/5 – 15/10. 100 places.
Tel: 98 73 31 22.

Ploëmel 56400
*** *Kergo*. Open 15/6 – 15/9. 135 places. Tel: 97 56 80 66.

Plogoff 29113
** *Pointe Du Raz Camping*. Open 1/5 – 15/9. 35 places.

Tel: 98 70 62 94.

Plomeur 29120

   *** *La Pointe de la Torche*. Open Easter – 31/10. 121 places.
Tel: 98 58 62 82.

Plomodiern 29550

   *** *L'Iroise*. Open 1/4 – 30/9. 132 places.
Tel: 98 81 52 72.

Plonévez-Porzay 29550

   **** *International de Kervel*. Open 1/5 – 15/9. 250 places.
Pool. Tel: 98 92 51 54.

   ** *Treguer Plage*. Open 1/6 – 15/9. 333 places.
Tel: 98 92 53 52.

   ** *Sainte Anne*. Open Easter – 15/9. 100 places.
Tel: 98 92 51 17.

Plouescat 29430

   ** *Municipal Kernic Ty*. Open 15/6 – 31/8. 155 places.
Tel: 98 69 86 60.

Plouézec 22470

   *** *Le Cap Horn*. Open 1/6 – 10/9. 100 places.
Tel: 96 20 64 28.

Plouézoc'h 29252

   *** *Baie de Térénez*. Open Easter – 30/9. 165 places. Pool.
Tel: 98 67 26 80.

Plougasnou 29630

   ** *Municipal Primel Tregastel*. Open Easter – 30/9. 120
places. Tel: 98 72 37 06.

Plougastel-Daoulas 29470

   ** *Saint-Jean*. Open all year. 120 places. Tel: 98 40 32 90.

Plouguerneau 29880

   ** *Municipal la Grève Blanche*. Open 15/6 – 15/9. 100 places.
Tel: 98 04 70 35.

Plouha 22580

   **** *Domaine de Kéravel*. Open Easter – 30/9. 90 places.
Pool. Tel: 96 22 49 13.

Plouharnel 56720

   *** *Kersily*. Open 25/3 – 15/10. 120 places.

Tel: 97 52 39 65.

*** *L'Étang de Loperhet*. Open 1/4 – 31/10. 165 places.
Tel: 97 52 34 68.

*** *Les Bruyères*. Open Easter – 30/10. 105 places.
Tel: 97 52 30 57.

** *Municipal les Sables Blancs*. Open Easter – 30/9. 565 places. Tel: 97 52 37 15.

Plouhinec 56680

*** *Le Monténo*. Open 1/4 – 30/10. 230 places.
Tel: 97 36 76 63.

Plozevet 29710

** *Cornouaille*. Open 15/6 – 30/9. 100 places. Pool.
Tel: 98 91 30 81

Pont l'Abbé 29120

*** *L'Écureuil*. Open 15/6 – 15/9. 100 places.
Tel: 98 87 03 39.

Pont-Réan 35580

*** *Base Nautique*. Open 1/4 – 30/9. 60 places.
Tel: 99 42 21 91.

Port-Louis 56290

** *Municipal Les Remparts*. Open 15/6 – 15/9. 135 places.
Tel: 97 82 47 16.

Le Pouldu/Clohars-Carnoët 29121

** *Kéranquernat*. Open Easter – 30/9. 100 places.
Tel: 98 39 92 32.

Poullan-sur-Mer 29100

**** *Le Pil-Koad*. Open 1/4 – 30/9. 110 places. Pool.
Tel: 98 74 26 39.

Quiberon 56170

*** *Beauséjour*. Open 1/4 – 30/9. 150 places.
Tel: 97 30 44 93.

*** *Domisilami*. Open 15/3 – 5/11. 170 places.
Tel: 97 50 22 52.

** *Municipal de Bois d'Amour*. Open 1/5 – 30/9. 335 places.
Tel: 97 50 13 52.

** *Municipal Goviro*. Open all year. 200 places.

Tel: 97 50 13 54.

Quimper 29000
   **** *L'Orangerie de Lanniron*. Open 1/5 – 15/9. 100 places.
   Pool. Tel: 98 90 62 02.

Rennes 35000
   ** *Municipal les Gayeulles*. Open 25/3 – 2/10. 100 places.
   Tel: 99 36 91 22.

Riec-sur-Belon 29340
   ** *De Belon*. Open 1/3 – 15/11. 150 places.
   Tel: 98 06 41 43.

La Roche-Bernard 56130
   *** *Municipal le Patis*. Open 15/3 – 31/10. 60 places.
   Tel: 99 90 60 13.

Rochefort-en-Terre 56220
   ** *Municipal le Chemin de Bogeais*. Open 1/6 – 30/9. 100
   places. Tel: 97 43 32 81.

Roscoff 29680
   ** *Manoir de Kérestat*. Open all year. 45 places.
   Tel: 98 69 71 92.
   ** *Municipal Penharidy*. Open Easter – 30/9. 200 places.
   Tel: 98 69 70 86.

Saint-Briac-sur-Mer 35800
   *** *L'Emeraude*. Open Easter – 30/9. 200 places.
   Tel: 99 88 34 55.
   ** *Municipal le Pont Lorrain*. Open 1/7 – 10/9. 100 places.
   Tel: 99 88 34 64.

Saint-Brieuc 22000
   ** *Municipal Brezillet*. Open all year. 100 places.
   Tel: 96 78 66 87.

Saint-Cast-le-Guildo 22380
   **** *Le Châtelet*. Open 1/5 – 20/9. 170 places.
   Tel: 96 41 96 33.
   ** *La Ferme de Pen Guen*. Open Easter – 30/9. 300 places.
   Tel: 96 41 92 18.
   ** *Municipal les Mielles*. Open 1/5 – 15/9. 220 places.
   Tel: 96 41 87 60.

Saint-Evarzec 29170

   *** *Keromen*. Open 1/7 – 31/8. 80 places. Tel: 98 56 20 63.

Saint-Gildas-de-Rhuys 56730

   *** *Le Menhir*. Open 15/6 – 15/9. 180 places. Pool.
Tel: 97 45 22 88.

   ** *Les Govelins*. Open Easter – 15/9. 100 places. Pool.
Tel: 97 45 21 67.

Saint-Jacut-de-la-Mer 22750

   ** *Municipal la Manchette*. Open Easter – 30/9. 374 places.
Tel: 96 27 70 33.

Saint-Lunaire 35800

   *** *La Touesse*. Open 27/3 – 10/9. 100 places.
Tel: 99 46 61 13.

Saint-Malo 35400

   **** *Le P'tit Bois*. Open 15/5 – 15/9. 180 places. Pool.
Tel: 99 81 48 36.

   ** *La Fontaine*. Open 15/6 – 15/9. 100 places.
Tel: 99 81 62 62.

   ** *Municipal Cité d'Aleth*. Open all year. 400 places.
Tel: 99 81 60 91.

   ** *Municipal le Nicet*. Open 1/5 – 20/9. 250 places.
Tel: 99 40 26 32.

Saint-Michel-en-Grève 22300

   **** *Les Capucines*. Open 15/5 – 15/9. 50 places. Pool.
Tel: 96 35 72 28.

Saint-Père-Marc-en-Poulet 35430

   *** *Bel Event*. Open 1/6 – 31/8. 96 places. Pool.
Tel: 99 58 83 79.

Saint-Philibert 56470

   *** *Au Vieux Logis*. Open Easter – 30/9. 90 places.
Tel: 97 55 01 17.

   *** *Le Chat Noir*. Open 15/6 – 15/9. 97 places.
Tel: 97 55 04 90.

Saint-Pierre-Quiberon 56510

   *** *Parc Er Lann*. Open 15/5 – 15/9. 135 places.
Tel: 97 50 24 93.

** *Municipal de Penthièvre*. Open 25/3 – 3/9. 665 places.
Tel: 97 52 33 86.
** *Port Blanc*. Open 15/6 – 15/9. 150 places.
Tel: 97 30 91 30.

Saint-Pol-de-Léon 29250

** *Municipal Trologot*. Open 20/5 – 30/9. 114 places.
Tel: 98 69 06 26.
** *Ar Kleguer*. Open 1/4 – 30/9. 70 places. Pool.
Tel: 98 69 18 81.

Saint-Quay-Portrieux 22410

*** *Belle Vue*. Open 1/5 – 15/9. 200 places.
Tel: 96 70 41 84.

Saint-Samson-sur-Rance 22100

*** *Municipal Beausejour*. Open 15/6 – 15/9. 120 places.
Tel: 96 39 53 27.

Saint-Yvi 29140

*** *Coatmor*. Open 15/6 – 15/9. 95 places.
Tel: 98 94 71 25.
*** *Municipal Bois de Pleuven*. Open Easter – 30/9. 354
places. Pool. Tel: 98 94 70 47.

Sainte-Anne-d'Auray 56400

** *Municipal le Motten*. Open 15/6 – 15/9. 100 places.
Tel: 97 57 60 27.

Sarzeau 56370

**** *La Madone*. Open 15/5 – 15/9. 380 places.
Tel: 97 67 33 30.
*** *Kersial*. Open 1/6 – 30/9. 100 places. Tel: 97 41 75 59.
*** *Les Genêts*. Open 15/6 – 15/9. 125 places. Pool.
Tel: 97 41 87 22.
*** *Le Bohat*. Open 20/5 – 17/9. 225 places. Pool.
Tel: 97 41 78 68.
*** *Le Treste*. Open 6/6 – 20/9. 190 places.
Tel: 97 41 79 60.

Séné 56860

*** *Moulin de Cantizac*. Open 15/4 – 15/11. 100 places.
Tel: 97 66 90 26.

Taupont-Ploërmel 56800
   *** *Vallée du Ninian*. Open 15/3 – 30/10. 40 places.
   Tel: 97 93 53 01.

Telgruc-sur-Mer 29560
   *** *Le Panoramic*. Open 15/5 – 20/9. 220 places. Pool.
   Tel: 98 27 78 41.

Theix 56450
   *** *Rhuys*. Open 1/5 – 30/9. 50 places. Tel: 97 54 14 77.
   ** *La Poupleraie*. Open 15/6 – 15/10. 100 places.
   Tel: 97 43 09 46.

Le Tour-du-Parc 56370
   *** *Le Cadran Solaire*. Open 1/4 – 30/10. 115 places.
   Tel: 97 67 30 40.

Trébeurden 22560
   *** *Kerdual*. Open 1/5 – 30/9. 35 places. Tel: 96 23 54 86.

Trégastel 22730
   *** *Tourony*. Open 1/6 – 30/9. 100 places.
   Tel: 96 23 86 61.
   *** *Le Golven*. Open 1/5 – 15/9. 160 places.
   Tel: 96 23 87 77.

Trégunc 29910
   *** *Le Pendruc*. Open 20/6 – 10/9. 170 places. Pool.
   Tel: 98 97 66 28.

Trélévern 22660
   *** *Port l'Epine*. Open 29/4 – 23/9. 120 places.
   Tel: 96 23 71 94.

Trévou-Tréguignec 22660
   *** *Le Mat*. Open 15/6 – 15/9. 70 places.
   Tel: 96 23 71 52.

La Trinité-sur-Mer 56470
   **** *La Baie*. Open 20/5 – 16/9. 170 places. Pool.
   Tel: 97 55 73 42.
   **** *La Plage*. Open 23/5 – 15/9. 200 places.
   Tel: 97 55 73 28.
   *** *Kermarquer*. Open 1/6 – 15/9. 90 places.
   Tel: 97 55 79 18.

*** *Kervilor*. Open 1/6 – 15/9. 200 places. Pool.
Tel: 97 55 76 75.

*** *Park Plijadur*. Open 1/6 – 15/9. 198 places. Pool.
Tel: 97 55 72 05.

Le Val-André/Pléneuf 22370

*** *Le Minihy*. Open Easter – 15/9. 65 places.
Tel: 96 72 22 95.

*** *Municipal les Monts Colleux*. Open Easter – 30/9. 300
places. Tel: 96 72 95 10.

Vannes 56000

*** *Municipal de Conleau*. Open 1/4 – 30/9. 290 places.
Tel: 97 63 13 88.

Vitré 35500

** *Municipal Saint-Etienne*. Open all year. 50 places.
Tel: 99 75 25 28.

Le Vivier-sur-Mer 35960

** *Municipal l'Abri des Flots*. Open 1/4 – 30/9. 70 places.
Tel: 99 48 91 57.

N.B. Although La Baule is no longer officially in Brittany,
some campsites in this popular resort have been included.

CASTLES

(Consult local Tourist Offices for days and times)

COTES-DU-NORD

Erquy

Bienassis Castle: Fortified castle, 15th to 17th century.
Drawing-rooms, guard-room, ramparts, moat and formal
gardens.

Fréhel

Fréhel Castle: 12th to 15th century. Chapel. ramparts, belfry,
dungeons, cannonball furnace.

Lanvellec
Rosanbo Castle: 14th century. Fine Louis XIV staircase and furniture. Reading room and gardens.

Plédéliac
La Hunaudaye Castle: 14th to 15th-century ruined fortress.

Ploubezré
Kergrist Castle: One of the most beautiful houses in the Trégor region.

Ploézal
La Roche-Jagu Castle: 15th-century fortified castle on the Trieux estuary. Restored in recent years it is now a cultural centre with art exhibitions, concerts, children's entertainments and other activities in summer.

Quintin
Quintin Castle: 17th – 18th century. Exterior only open.

Trébry-Moncontour
La Touche-Trébry Castle: 16th-century turretted Renaissance château with central courtyard.

Tonquédec
Tonquédec Castle: 15th-century fortified castle with turrets and massive walls. Wonderful view of the valley below. Horse-drawn carriage rides round the grounds.

FINISTERE

Loctudy
Kérazan Castle: 16th century. Fine collection of French paintings inc. Breton life.

Plouzévédé
Kerjean Castle: 16th century. Beautiful Breton furniture, park and fountain.

Saint-Goazec

Trévarez Castle: Exterior only. Rhododendron garden.

Saint-Pol-de-Léon
Kérouzéré Castle: 15th century. Restored in 1602.

ILLE-ET-VILAINE

Antrain-sur-Couesnon
Bonnefontaine Castle: 11th century. Restored in 1859. Only exterior and park open.

Bécherel
Caradeuc Castle: Early 18th century. Beautiful views over the Rance valley. Exterior, park and gardens open.

Châteaugiron
Châteaugiron Castle: Medieval castle overlooking ancient little town. *Son-et-lumière* in summer.

Combourg
Combourg Castle: 11th to 15th century. Chateaubriand spent part of his youth here. One of the best preserved of the feudal castles.

Fougères
Fougères Castle: 11th century dominating town below. One of the largest fortified castles in Europe. 13 turrets, ramparts, garden.

Montauban
Montauban-de-Bretagne Castle: 12th- and 18th-century feudal castle. Interior with medieval furniture, arms, suits of armour and dungeon.

Montmuran
Montmuran Castle: 12th century. Ancient gate tower and drawbridge.

Pleugueneuc

Bourbansais Castle: 16th to 18th century. Interior, formal gardens and small zoo.

Saint-Malo
Saint-Malo Castle: 15th century. Situated at the eastern end of the walled town. Four large towers, dungeon, museum and waxworks.

Vitré
Vitré Castle: 11th to 15th century. Imposing granite feudal castle overlooking one of the best preserved medieval towns in France. Massive walls, towers housing museum, 16th-century chapel and loggia. *Son-et-lumière.*

MORBIHAN

Allaire-Béganne
Estier Castle: 16th century. Numerous superb fireplaces.

Béganne
De Lehélec Castle: 16th – 17th century. Impressive residence in pink and grey granite. Good collection of antique furniture.

Bignan
De Kerguéhennec Castle: Restored castle and wooded park. Permanent exhibition of contemporary sculpture.

Le Guerno-Musillac
De Brandféré Castle: 14th to 19th century. 85 acre wildlife park and zoo. Painting exhibitions.

Josselin
De Rohan Castle: 11th to 14th century. A story-book castle. Its great walls rise sheer from the road below and its three circular pointed towers are reflected in the river Oust. Within the ramparts a *corps de logis* building with pinnacles, gables and balustrades. The ground floor rooms were wonderfully restored in the 19th century.

Pontivy
Pontivy Castle: 15th century. Well preserved fortress.
Exhibition centre. Music festivals in summer.

Rochefort-en-Terre
Rochefort-en-Terre Castle: 12th to 20th century. Overlooks
medieval town. Contains a regional museum.

Sarzeau
De Suscinio Castle: 13th to 16th century. Military fortress.
Former home of the Dukes of Brittany. Splendid medieval
floor in ducal chapel. Festival in summer.

Theix
Plessis-Josso Castle: 14th to 16th century. Fortified manor
house, pavilion, watermill and woodland.

Vannes
Gaillard Castle: 15th century. Splendid manor house which
was the seat of Brittany's first parliament. Prehistoric
museum.

GOLF COURSES

(For further information, fees, facilities, etc., contact
individual clubs)

COTES-DU-NORD

Golf les Ajoncs d'Or, Kergrain Lantique, St-Quay-Portrieux
22410. Tel: 96 71 90 74.
Situated 6 km from Saint-Quay-Portrieux, an attractive
seaside town with sandy beaches, numerous moorings, tennis
courts, swimming-pool, casino and cinema. 18 holes. Weekly
tickets available.
Golf de Boisgelin, Château de Coatguelen, Pléhédel, Lanvollon
22290. Tel: 96 22 31 24.

Situated 10 km from Paimpol a small fishing-port which makes an ideal centre for excursions. 18 holes. Guests at the Château hotel have priority.

Golf de Saint-Samson, Pleumeur-Bodou 22560.

Tel: 96 23 87 34.

Situated 4 km from Trégastel. Nearby good beaches, sailing, tennis, riding, fishing and trips to the islands. 18 holes. Competitions open to visitors.

Golf de Sables d'Or, Fréhel 22240. Tel: 96 41 42 57.

Situated at Sables-d'Or-les-Pins with its fine sands and excellent bathing, windsurfing, sailing and tennis. 9 holes. Competitions open to visitors.

Golf de Pen-Guen, Saint-Cast-Le-Guildo, Saint-Cast 22380. Tel: 96 41 91 20.

Situated in a pretty little resort set on the end of a peninsula on the Emerald Coast. 9 holes. Competitions open to visitors.

FINISTERE

Golf de l'Odet, Bénodet 29950. Tel: 98 54 87 88.

Situated 4 km from the ever-popular seaside resort of Bénodet and 12 km from the medieval town of Quimper. 18- and 9-hole courses.

Golf de Cornouaille, La Forêt-Fouesnant 29940.

Tel: 98 56 97 09.

Situated at La Forêt-Fouesnant a small village set amongst apple orchards with a picturesque bay. 9 holes. Competitions open to visitors. Handicap certificate required.

Golf d'Iroise, Parc des Loisirs de Lannrohou, Saint-Urbain, Landerneau 29800. Tel: 98 85 16 17.

Situated 7 km from the pretty market town of Landerneau. 18 holes and 9 holes. Sunday competitions open to visitors.

ILLE-ET-VILAINE

Golf de Dinard, Saint-Briac 35800. Tel: 99 88 32 07.

Situated 6 km from the elegant resort of Dinard, popular with the British since Victorian times and offering a wide range of seaside and leisure activities. 18 holes. Handicap certificate required. Often crowded at weekends.

Golf de Saint-Malo-le-Tronchet, Miniac-Morvan 35540.
Tel: 99 58 96 69.
Situated 12 km from the beautifully preserved medieval town of Dinan and not far from the excellent beaches of the north Brittany coast. 18 and 9 holes.

Golf de Rennes, Saint-Jaques de la Lande 35136.
Tel: 99 64 24 18.
Situated 8 km from Rennes, the cultural capital of Brittany, and within easy driving distance of several interesting châteaux. 18 holes.

Golf de la Freslonniere, Le Rheu, 35650. Tel: 99 60 84 09.
Situated 3 km from Rennes. 18 holes.

Golf de Chateau des Ormes, Dol-de-Bretagne 35120.
Tel: 99 48 40 27.
Situated 8 km from the ancient town of Dol. 18 holes.

MORBIHAN

Golf de Saint-Laurent, Ploemel, Auray 56400.
Tel: 97 56 85 18.
Close to fine beaches and the Thalassotherapy Centre at Carnac, this is an ideal place for a golfing, health and fitness holiday. Carnac is famous throughout the world for its prehistoric standing stones – the largest site in Brittany. 18 holes and 9 holes.

Golf de Sauzon, Belle-Ile-en-Mer 56360. Tel: 97 31 64 65.
Situated on the largest of Brittany's off-shore islands Belle-Ile-en-Mer. Delightful island with sheltered creeks for good bathing and many small villages of whitewashed houses. Centre for international yachting events. Reached by ferry from Quiberon. 18 holes. Clubhouse once Sarah Bernhardt's farm.

Golf du Kervert, Saint-Gildas-de-Rhuys 56730.
Tel: 97 45 30 09.
Situated near the tiny resort of Le Crouesty at the tip of the
Rhuys Peninsula with many good beaches and famous
châteaux. 18 holes.
Golf de Baden, Baden 56870. Tel: 97 57 18 96.
Near to small fishing-port and close to the beaches of the Gulf
of Morbihan. Boat trips to the offshore islands. 18 holes.

The department of Loire–Atlantique is no longer officially in
Brittany. However, this list would be incomplete without
these two famous courses –
St-Denac, La Baule 44500. Tel: 40 60 46 18.
A championship 18-hole course a few km from the
sophisticated resort of La Baule.
La Bretesche, Missillac 44780. Tel: 40 88 30 03.
One of France's most famous courses in a lovely château
setting. 24 km from Redon. 18 holes.

HOTELS

Apply direct to hotels for current rates. The address should
read as follows – name of the hotel followed by the town and
Department number.
(Street names are not necessary except where given.) The first
two digits of the number indicate the Department: 22 = Côtes-
du-Nord; 29 = Finistère; 35 = Ille-et-Vilaine; 56 = Morbihan.

DB = facilities for disabled.

Aberwrach 29870
    ** *Baie des Anges*. Open Easter – 31/10. 17 rooms. Garden.
    Sea View. DB. Tel: 98 04 90 04

Allaire 56350
    ** *Le Gaudence*. Open all year 17 rooms. Garden.
    Tel: 99 71 93 64.

Arradon 56610

** *Hespérie*. Open all year. 25 rooms. Garden. DB.
Tel: 97 44 72 25.

Arzon-Port-Navalo 56640

** *Rhuys*. Open 1/4 – 30/9. 14 rooms. Garden. Sea view.
Tel: 97 53 70 01.

Audierne 29770

*** *le Goyen*. Open all year. 34 rooms. Port view. DB.
Tel: 98 70 08 88.

**Roi Gradlon*. Open 1/3 – 15/1. 20 rooms. View of the
port. DB. Tel: 98 70 04 51.

Auray 56400

** *De la Marie*. Open all year. 21 rooms. Tel: 97 24 04 65.

** *Du Loch*. Open all year. 30 rooms. Garden. DB.
Tel: 97 56 48 33.

** *Le Branhoc*. Open all year. 28 rooms. Garden. DB.
Tel: 97 56 41 55.

Baden 56870

** *Le Gavrinis*. Open all year. 19 rooms. Garden.
Tel: 97 57 00 82.

Bain-de-Bretagne 35470

* *Des Quatre Vents*. Open 16/1 – 21/12. 20 rooms.
Tel: 99 43 71 49.

Bannalec 29380

* *La Crémaillere*. Open all year. 10 rooms.
Tel: 98 39 55 34.

La Baule 44500

**** *Hermitage*. Open 15/4 – 15/10. 237 rooms. Swimming-
pool. Garden. Tennis. Sea view. DB.
Tel: 40 60 37 00.

**** *Royal*. Open all year. 104 rooms. Tennis. Swimming-
pool. Garden. Sea view. DB. Tel: 40 60 33 06.

*** *Alexandra*. Open 1/3 – 1/10. 36 rooms. Sea view. DB.
Tel: 40 60 30 06.

*** *Bellevue-Plage*. Open 5/2 – 12/11. 34 rooms. Sea view.
Tel: 40 60 28 55.

** *Concorde*. Open Easter – 1/10. 47 rooms. Garden. Sea view. Tel: 40 60 23 09.

** *Bretagne*. Open all year. 25 rooms. Sea view.
Tel: 40 60 21 92.

** *La Palmeraie*. Open Easter – 1/10. 23 rooms. Garden.
Tel: 40 60 24 41.

** *Mariza*. Open 1/2 – 1/11. 24 rooms. Sea view.
Tel: 40 60 20 21.

** *Riviera*. Open 1/5 – 10/10. 20 rooms. Garden.
Tel: 40 60 28 97.

** *Welcome*. Open 20/3 – 15/10. 18 rooms. Sea view.
Tel: 40 60 30 25.

Belle-Ile-en-Mer (Island of) 56360

**** *Castel Clara (Bangor)*. Open 15/3 – 31/12. 32 rooms.
Tennis. Swimming-pool. Garden. Sea view. DB.
Tel: 97 31 84 21.

*** *Le Cardinal (Sauzon)*. Open 1/4 – 1/10. 85 rooms. Sea view. Tel: 97 31 61 60.

*** *Manoir de Goulphar (Bangor)*. Open 23/3 – 5/11. 52 rooms. Garden. Sea view. Tel: 97 31 80 10.

** *Bretagne (Le Palais)*. Open all year. 29 rooms. Sea view.
Tel: 97 31 80 14.

Belle-Isle-en-Terre 22810

** *Le Relais de L'Argoat*. Open 1/3 – 30/1. 10 rooms.
Tel: 96 43 00 34.

Bénodet 29950

**** *Gwel Kaer*. Open 1/2 – 15/12. 24 rooms. Sea view.
DB. Tel: 98 57 04 38.

*** *Ker Moor et Kastel Moor*. Open Easter – 30/9. 83 rooms.
Swimming-pool. Tennis. Garden. Sea view.
Tel: 98 57 04 48.

*** *Menez-Frost*. Open Easter – 15/10. 56 rooms. Tennis.
Swimming-pool. Garden. DB. Tel: 98 57 03 09.

** *Armoric*. Open 15/5 – 15/9 38 rooms. Garden. DB.
Tel: 98 57 04 03.

** *L'Ancre de Marine.* Open 15/3 – 5/11. 25 rooms. Sea view. Tel: 98 57 05 29.

** *De la Poste.* Open all year. 36 rooms. Port view. DB. Tel: 98 57 01 09.

** *Des Bains.* Open Easter – 15/11. 30 rooms. Garden. Sea view. Swimming-pool. Tel: 98 57 03 41.

** *Le Cornouaille.* Open 1/5 – 30/9. 30 rooms. Garden. Tel: 98 57 03 78.

Billiers 56190

**** *Domaine de Rochevilaine.* Open 20/2 – 31/12. 27 rooms. Swimming-pool. Garden. Sea view. DB. Tel: 97 41 69 27.

Brest 29200

*** *Ajoncs d'Or.* (*1 Rue Amiral Nicol.*) Open all year. 17 rooms. Tennis. Garden. DB. Tel: 98 45 12 42.

*** *Novotel.* (*Zac de Kergaradec.*) Open all year. 85 rooms. Swimming-pool. Garden. DB. Tel: 98 02 32 83.

** *France.* (*1 Ave Amiral Reveillère*). Open all year. 40 rooms. Garden. Sea view. Tel 98 46 18 88.

** *Climat de France.* (*Rue Romain des Fosses.*) Open all year. 46 rooms. Garden. DB. Tel: 98 47 50 50.

** *Vauban.* (*17 Ave Clémenceau.*) Open all year. 53 rooms. Sea view. DB. Tel: 98 46 06 88.

Brignogan-Plages 29890

** *Hostellerie Castel Regis.* Open Easter – 30/9. 17 rooms. Tennis. Swimming-pool. Garden. Sea view. DB. Tel: 98 83 40 22.

Camaret-sur-Mer 29570

** *France.* Open 1/4 – 11/11. 22 rooms. Sea view. DB. Tel: 98 27 93 06.

** *Styvel.* Open 15/3 – 15/11. 14 rooms. Sea view. Tel: 98 27 92 74.

Cancale 35260

*** *Continental.* Open 15/3 – 16/12. 18 rooms. Sea view. Tel: 99 89 60 16.

** *Pointe du Grouin.* Open 1/4 – 30/9. 18 rooms. Sea view.

Tel: 99 89 60 55.

** *Emeraude*. Open 20/12 – 15/11. 18 rooms. Garden. Sea view. Tel: 99 89 61 76.

Carantec 29660

* *Falaise*. Open Easter – 20/9. 24 rooms. Garden. Sea view. Tel: 98 67 00 53.

Carnac 56340

**** *Diana*. Open 29/4 – 9/10. 33 rooms. Tennis. Garden. Sea view. DB. Tel: 97 52 05 38.

*** *Novotel*. Open 1/2 – 31/12. 110 rooms. Swimming-pool. Garden. View of port. DB. Tel: 97 52 53 00.

*** *Résidence Orion*. Open all year. 79 rooms. Tennis. Garden. DB. Tel: 97 52 22 68.

** *Armoric*. Open Easter – 15/9. 25 rooms. Tennis. Garden. Tel: 97 52 13 47.

** *Chez Nous*. Open Easter – 30/10. 20 rooms. Garden. Tel: 97 52 07 28.

** *Marine*. Open 15/2 – 30/11. 33 rooms. Garden. Tel: 97 52 07 33.

** *Celtique*. Open 1/2 – 31/10. 35 rooms. Garden. DB. Tel: 97 52 11 49.

** *Alignements*. Open 15/4 – 20/9. 27 rooms. Garden. Tel: 97 52 06 30.

Cesson-Sévigné 35510

** *Valette*. Open all year. 20 rooms. Garden. Tel: 99 83 22 49.

** *Floréal*. Open all year. 51 rooms. Garden. DB. Tel: 99 83 82 82.

Châteaubourg 35220

*** *Ar Milin*. Open 2/1 – 20/12. 33 rooms. Tennis. Garden. DB. Tel: 99 00 30 91.

Châteaugiron 35410

* *Cheval Blanc et Château*. Open all year. 18 rooms. Tel: 99 37 40 27.

Châteaulin 29150

** *Bon Accueil*. Open 1/2 – 31/12. 59 rooms. Garden. View of port. DB. Tel: 98 86 15 77.

Châteauneuf-du-Faou 29520

* *Gai Logis*. Open all year. 12 rooms. Tel: 98 81 73 87.

Combourg 35270

** *Du Château*. Open 25/1 – 15/12. 31 rooms. Garden. View of port. DB. Tel: 99 73 00 38.

** *Du Lac*. Open all year. 30 rooms. Garden. View of lake. Tel: 99 73 05 65.

Concarneau 29900

**** *Belle Etoile*. Open 1/3 – 31/12. 30 rooms. Tennis. Garden. Sea view. DB. Tel: 98 97 05 73.

*** *Ty Chupen Gwenn*. Open all year. 15 rooms. Garden. Sea view. Tel: 98 97 01 43.

*** *De L'Océan*. Open all year. 40 rooms. Swimming-pool. Garden. Sea view. DB. Tel: 98 50 53 50.

** *Grand*. Open Easter – 1/10. 33 rooms. Sea view. Tel: 98 97 00 28.

** *Sables Blancs*. Open 27/3 – 2/11. 48 rooms. Garden. Sea view. DB. Tel: 98 97 01 39.

** *Modern*. Open all year. 19 rooms. Tel: 98 97 03 36.

Le Conquet 29217

** *Pointe Ste-Barbe*. Open 6/2 – 2/1. 33 rooms. Sea view. DB. Tel: 98 89 00 26.

** *Marianna*. Open Easter – 31/10. 28 rooms. Garden. Sea view. DB. Tel: 98 48 30 02.

Crozon Morgat 29160

** *Hostellerie de la Mer*. Open all year. 25 rooms. Sea view. DB. Tel: 98 27 61 65.

** *De la Ville D'Ys*. Open Easter – 30/9. 42 rooms. Sea view. Tel: 98 27 06 49.

** *Moderne*. Open all year. 37 rooms. Tel: 98 27 00 10.

Dinan 22100

*** *D'Avaugour*. Open all year. 27 rooms. Garden. DB. Tel: 96 39 07 49.

** *France*. Open all year. 14 rooms. Tel: 96 39 22 56.

** *Des Alleux (Taden)*. Open all year. 36 rooms. Garden.
DB. Tel: 96 85 16 10.

Dinard 35800

**** *Grand*. Open Easter – 1/10. 100 rooms. Garden. Sea
view. Swimming-pool. DB. Tel: 99 46 10 28.

*** *Crystal*. Open all year. 26 rooms. Sea view. DB.
Tel: 99 46 66 71.

** *Climat de France*. Open all year. 40 rooms. Garden. Sea
view. Swimming-pool. DB. Tel: 99 46 69 55.

** *Des Bains*. Open 15/3 – 15/10. 39 rooms. Sea view. DB.
Tel: 99 46 13 71.

** *Mont St Michel*. Open 15/3 – 15/11. 27 rooms. Garden.
DB. Tel: 99 46 10 40.

** *Emeraude Plage*. Open 1/4 – 30/9. 59 rooms. Garden. Sea
view. DB. Tel: 99 46 15 79.

** *La Plage*. Open 15/3 – 31/1. 18 rooms. Sea view.
Tel: 99 46 14 87.

** *Vieux Manoir*. Open 1/3 – 15/11. 37 rooms. Garden. DB.
Tel: 99 46 14 69.

** *Les Tilleuls*. Open all year. 32 rooms. Garden.
Tel: 99 46 18 06.

** *Résidence les Pins*. Open all year. 13 rooms. Tennis.
Swimming-pool. Garden. DB. Tel: 99 46 13 99.

Dol-de-Bretagne 35120

** *Logis de la Breiz Arthur*. Open all year. 24 rooms.
Garden. Tel: 99 48 02 89.

* *De Bretagne*. Open all year. 29 rooms. Garden.
Tel: 99 48 02 03.

Douarnenez 29100

** *Auberge de Kerveoc'h*. Open Easter – 15/10. 14 rooms.
Garden. Tel: 98 92 07 58.

** *Grand de la Plage*. Open all year. 105 rooms. Sea view.
DB. Tel: 98 74 00 21.

** *Bretagne*. Open all year. 27 rooms. DB.
Tel: 98 92 30 44.

Erdeven 56410

** *Auberge du Sous Bois*. Open 15/3 – 15/10. 22 rooms.
Garden. Tel: 97 55 66 10.

** *Voyageurs*. Open 1/4 – 30/9. 20 rooms. Tel: 97 55 64 47.

Erquy 22430

** *De la Plage*. Open 1/2 – 15/11. 26 rooms. Sea view.
Tel: 96 72 30 09.

Le Faou 29580

** *Vielle Renommée*. Open all year. 38 rooms. DB.
Tel: 98 81 90 31.

** *De la Place*. Open all year. 35 rooms. Tel: 98 81 91 19.

La Forêt-Fouesnant 29940

**** *Manoir du Stang*. Open 1/5 – 30/9. 28 rooms. Tennis.
Garden. Tel: 98 56 97 37.

** *De la Baie*. Open all year. 20 rooms. Sea view.
Tel: 98 56 97 35.

** *Espérance*. Open 25/3 – 30/9. 30 rooms. Garden. Sea
view. Tel: 98 56 96 58.

Fouesnant 29170

** *Belle Vue*. *(Cap-Coz)* Open 15/3 – 30/10. 21 rooms.
Garden. Sea view. Tel: 98 56 00 33.

** *Celtique (Cap-Coz)*. Open 1/5 – 30/9. 47 rooms. Garden.
Sea view. Tel: 98 56 01 79.

** *De la Pointe Cap-Coz*. Open 1/4 – 30/9. 22 rooms. Sea
view. Tel: 98 56 01 63.

** *De la Pointe de Mousterlin*. Open 1/5 – 30/9. 67 rooms.
Tennis. Garden. Sea view. DB. Tel: 98 56 04 12.

** *Roudou*. Open Easter – 30/9. 20 rooms. Garden.
Tel: 98 56 01 26.

** *Thalamot (Beg-Meil.)* Open 28/4 – 5/10. 34 rooms.
Garden. Sea view. Tel: 98 94 97 38.

* *Bretagne (Beg-Meil)* Open 20/3 – 30/9. 38 rooms. Garden.
DB. Tel: 98 94 98 04.

Fougères 35300

** *Voyageurs*. Open 4/1 – 20/12. 37 rooms. DB.
Tel: 99 99 18 21.

** *Mainotel.* Open all year. 50 rooms. Tennis. Garden. DB.
Tel: 99 99 81 55.

Guidel 56520

*** *Manoir la Chataigneraie.* Open all year. 10 rooms.
Garden. Tel: 97 65 99 93.

*** *Maeva.* Open all year. 37 rooms. Tennis. Swimming-
pool. Garden. DB. Sea view. Tel: 97 32 81 81.

Le Guilvinec 29730

** *Du Port.* Open 5/1 – 23/12. 40 rooms. Sea view.
Tel: 98 58 10 10.

Guingamp 22200

*** *Relais du Roy.* Open all year. 7 rooms.
Tel: 96 43 76 62

** *D'Armor.* Open all year. 23 rooms. DB.
Tel: 96 43 76 16.

** *Goeland.* Open all year. 30 rooms. Garden. DB.
Tel: 96 21 09 41.

Hennebont 56700

**** *Château de Locguenole.* Open 1/3 – 15/11. 35 rooms.
Tennis. Swimming-pool. Garden. Port view. DB.
Tel: 97 76 29 04.

** *Auberge de Toul Douar.* Open all year. 32 rooms. Garden.
Tel: 97 36 24 04.

Huelgoat 29690

* *Du Lac.* Open all year. 24 rooms. Garden. View of Port.
Tel: 98 99 71 14.

Ile-de Bréhat 22870

** *Bellevue.* Open 30/3 – 15/11. 18 rooms. Garden. Sea
view. DB. Tel: 96 20 00 05.

** *Vieille Auberge.* Open Easter – 6/11. 15 rooms. Garden.
DB. Tel: 96 20 00 24.

Ile de Groix 56590

** *La Marine.* Open all year. 22 rooms. Garden. Sea view.
Tel: 97 05 80 05.

Ile-Tudy 29980

** *Euromer*. Open 1/4 – 30/9. 62 rooms. Garden.
Swimming-pool. DB. Tel: 98 56 39 27.

Josselin 56120
** *Château*. Open 1/3 – 31/1. 36 rooms. View of port.
Tel: 97 22 20 11.
** *Relais de l'Oust*. Open all year. 25 rooms. Garden. DB.
Tel: 97 75 63 06.

Lamballe 22400
*** *Angleterre*. Open all year. 22 rooms. Tel: 96 31 00 16.
** *Tour d'Argent*. Open all year. 30 rooms. Garden.
Tel: 96 31 01 37.

Lampaul-Guimiliau 29400
** *De l'Enclos*. Open all year. 36 rooms. Garden. DB.
Tel: 98 68 77 08.

Landerneau 29800
** *Ibis*. Open all year. 42 rooms. Garden. DB.
Tel: 98 21 31 32.
** *Clos du Pontic*. Open all year. 38 rooms. Garden. DB.
Tel: 98 21 50 91.

Landivisiau 29400
** *Inter Hotel du Lion*. Open all year. 44 rooms. DB.
Tel: 98 68 00 11.

Lanester 56600
** *Kerous*. Open all year. 20 rooms. Tel: 97 76 05 21.

Lannion 22300
** *Climat de France*. Open all year. 47 rooms. Garden. DB.
Tel: 96 48 70 18.
* *Le Bretagne*. Open all year. 28 rooms. Tel: 96 37 00 33.

Larmor-Baden 56790
** *Auberge Parc Fétan*. Open 15/3 – 30/10. 36 rooms.
Garden. Sea view. Tel: 97 57 04 38.
** *Du Centre*. Open all year. 18 rooms. Sea view.
Tel: 97 57 04 68.

Larmor-Plage 56260
** *Beau Rivage*. Open 1/12 – 30/10. 18 rooms. Garden. Sea
view. Tel: 97 65 50 11.

* *Louisiane Confortel*. Open all year. 31 rooms. Garden. Port view. DB. Tel: 97 83 58 28.

Lesconil 29740

** *Atlantic*. Open all year. 23 rooms. Garden.
Tel: 98 87 81 06.

** *De la Plage*. Open Easter – 15/10. 28 rooms. Sea view.
DB. Tel: 98 87 80 05.

** *Du Port*. Open 11/5 – 25/9. 34 rooms. Tel: 98 87 81 07.

Lesneven 29260

** *Le Weekend*. Open 1/2–31/12. 12 rooms. Garden. Port view. DB. Tel: 98 25 40 57.

* *Breiz Izel*. Open 15/10 – 30/9. 24 rooms. Garden.
Tel: 98 83 12 33.

Locmariaquer 56740

** *Le Relais de Kerpenhir*. Open all year. 16 rooms. Garden.
DB. Tel: 97 57 31 20.

Locronan 29180

** *Au Fer à Chevel*. Open all year. 35 rooms. Garden. DB.
Tel: 98 91 70 67.

Loctudy 29750

** *Tudy*. Open Easter – 30/9. 9 rooms. Sea view.
Tel: 98 87 42 99.

* *De Bretagne*. Open 15/6 – 15/9. 15 rooms. Sea view.
Tel: 98 87 40 21.

Lorient 56100

*** *Mercure (31 Place Jules Ferry)*. Open all year. 58 rooms.
DB. Tel: 97 21 35 73.

*** *Novotel (Caudan)*. Open all year. 88 rooms. Swimming-pool. DB. Tel: 97 76 02 16.

** *Central (1 Rue de Cambry)*. Open all year. 27 rooms. DB.
Tel: 97 21 16 52.

** *Cléria (27 Bd. Franchet d'Espérey)*. Open all year. 36 rooms. DB. Tel: 97 21 04 59.

** *Astoria (3 Rue de Clisson)*. Open all year. 40 rooms.
Tel: 97 21 10 23.

** *Kerotel (Rond Point du Plénéno)*. Open all year. 37 rooms.
DB. Tel: 97 87 90 97.

** *Léopol (11 Rue Waldeck Rousseau)*. Open 5/1 – 24/12. 32
rooms. DB. Tel: 97 21 23 16.

** *Inter-Hotel du Centre (30 Rue Ducouedic)*. Open all year. 34
rooms. DB. Tel: 97 64 13 27.

Louargat 22540

** *Le Manoir du Cleuziou*. Open 1/3 – 1/11. 29 rooms.
Tennis. Swimming-pool. Garden. Tel: 96 43 14 90.

Loudéac 22600

** *De France*. Open all year. 40 rooms. Garden. DB.
Tel: 96 28 00 15.

Moëlan-sur-Mer 29350

**** *Auberge des Moulins du Duc*. Open 1/3 – 15/1. 27
rooms. Swimming-pool. Garden. Port view. DB.
Tel: 98 39 60 73.

**** *Manoir de Kertalg*. Open 1/4 – 10/11. 9 rooms.
Garden. Sea view. Tel: 98 39 77 77.

** *Le Kerfany*. Open all year. 53 rooms. Garden.
Tel: 98 71 00 46.

Montauban-de-Bretagne 35360

** *De France*. Open 20/1 – 20/12. 13 rooms.
Tel: 99 06 40 19.

** *La Hucherais*. Open all year. 14 rooms. DB.
Tel: 99 06 40 29.

Morlaix 29600

*** *Minimote*. Open 5/1 – 20/12. 22 rooms. Garden. DB.
Tel: 98 88 35 30.

** *d'Europe*. Open 20/1 – 20/12. 68 rooms.
Tel: 98 62 11 99.

** *Fontaine*. Open 23/3 – 15/2. 35 rooms. Garden. DB.
Tel: 98 62 09 55.

Muzillac 56190

* *Genêts d'Or*. Open all year. 10 rooms. Tel: 97 41 68 49.

Nantes 44000

**** *Sofitel (Bd. Alexandre)*. Open all year. 100 rooms.
Tennis. Swimming-pool. Garden. Port view. DB.
Tel: 40 47 61 03.

*** *Astoria (11 Rue de Richebourg)*. Open all year. 45 rooms.
DB. Tel: 40 74 39 90.

*** *La Lande St Martin (Route de Clisson)*. Open all year. 40
rooms. Garden. DB. Tel: 40 06 20 06.

*** *Novotel (Carquefou)*. Open all year. 98 rooms.
Swimming-pool. Garden. DB. Tel: 40 52 64 64.

** *Grande de Nantes (2 Rue Santeuil)*. Open all year. 43
rooms. DB. Tel: 40 73 46 68.

** *De la Duchesse Anne (3 Place de la Duchesse Anne)*. Open
all year. 74 rooms. Tel: 40 74 30 29.

** *Graslin (1 Rue Péron)*. Open all year. 47 rooms.
Tel: 40 69 72 91.

** *Terminus (3 Allee du Cdt. Charcot)*. Open all year. 36
rooms. Tel: 40 74 24 51.

Paimpol 22500

*** *Le Barbu*. Open all year. 20 rooms. Swimming-pool.
Garden. Sea view. DB. Tel: 96 55 86 98.

*** *Le Relais Brenner*. Open 1/3 – 1/1. 29 rooms. Garden.
Sea view. DB. Tel: 96 20 11 05.

** *De la Marne*. Open all year. 16 rooms. Tel: 96 20 82 16.

** *Du Goëlo*. Open all year. 32 rooms. Sea view. DB.
Tel: 96 20 82 74.

Paimpont 35380

** *Relais de Brocéliande*. Open all year. 18 rooms. Garden.
DB. Tel: 99 07 81 07.

Peillac 56220

** *Chez Antoine*. Open 1/3 – 31/1. 12 rooms. Garden.
Tel: 99 91 24 43.

Penestin 56760

*** *Loscolo*. Open 25/4 – 2/10. 16 rooms. Garden. Sea
view. DB. Tel: 99 90 31 90.

** *Le Cynthia*. Open all year. 11 rooms. Garden. Sea view.
DB. Tel: 99 90 33 05.

Perros-Guirec 22700

*** *Grand de Trestraou*. Open all year. 70 rooms. Garden. Sea view. DB. Tel: 96 23 24 05

*** *Printania*. Open all year. 39 rooms. Garden. Sea view. Tennis. DB. Tel: 96 23 21 00.

*** *Morgane*. Open 1/3 – 20/10. 32 rooms. Swimming-pool. Sea view. Garden. Tel: 96 23 22 80.

** *De France*. Open 1/4 – 1/11. 30 rooms. Garden. Sea view. Tel: 96 23 20 27.

** *Hermitage*. Open 15/5 – 15/9. 25 rooms. Garden. Tel: 96 23 21 22.

** *Ker Mor*. Open Easter – 30/9. 30 rooms. Garden. Sea view. Tel: 96 23 14 19.

** *Les Feux des Isles*. Open all year. 16 rooms. Tennis. Garden. Sea view. Tel: 96 23 22 94.

** *Les Sternes*. Open all year. 20 rooms. Garden. Sea view. DB. Tel: 96 91 03 38.

** *Saint Yves*. Open all year. 20 rooms. Tel: 96 23 21 31.

** *Résidence Pierre et Vacances*. Open 15/3 – 30/10. 101 rooms. Swimming-pool. Garden. Sea view. DB. Tel: 96 91 17 91.

Plancoët 22130

*** *Hostellerie Abbatiale*. Open all year. 61 rooms. Tennis. Garden. Swimming-pool. DB. Tel: 96 84 05 01.

Pleyben 29190

* *Auberge le Poisson Blanc*. Open all year. 8 rooms. Tel: 98 73 34 76.

Plestin-les-Grèves 22310

** *Des Voyageurs*. Open all year. 26 rooms. Tel: 96 35 62 12

Pleumeur-Bodou 22560

** *De St Samson*. Open all year. 34 rooms. Tennis. Swimming-pool. Garden. Sea view. DB. Tel: 96 23 87 34.

Pléven 22130

*** *Manoir de Vaumadeuc*. Open 20/3 – 5/1. 9 rooms. Garden. Swimming-pool. DB. Tel: 96 84 46 17.

Ploëmel 56400

*** *Fairway*. Open all year. 42 rooms. Tennis. Swimming-pool. DB. Tel: 97 56 88 88.

Ploëmeur 56270

** *Le Vivier*. Open all year. 14 rooms. Sea view.
Tel: 97 82 99 60.

** *Les Astéries*. Open all year. 36 rooms. DB.
Tel: 97 86 21 97.

Ploërmel 56800

*** *Le Cobh*. Open all year. 13 rooms. Garden. DB.
Tel: 97 74 00 49.

** *Du Commerce*. Open all year. 19 rooms.
Tel: 97 74 05 32.

Plogoff/Pointe du Raz 29770

** *De la Baie des Trépassés*. Open all year. 53 rooms.
Garden. Tennis. Sea view. Tel: 98 70 61 34.

Plonéour-Lanvern 29720

** *De la Mairie*. Open all year. 18 rooms. Garden.
Tel: 98 87 61 34.

Plouescat 29430

** *La Caravelle*. Open all year. 17 rooms. Tel: 98 69 61 75.

Plougasnou 29630

** *De France*. Open all year. 21 rooms. Garden. DB.
Tel: 98 67 30 15.

Plougastel-Daoulas 29470

** *Kastel Roc'h*. Open all year. 45 rooms. Swimming-pool.
Garden. Tel: 98 40 32 00

Ploumanac'h 22700

** *Du Phare*. Open 30/5 – 30/9. 24 rooms. Sea view.
Garden. DB. Tel: 96 23 23 08.

** *St Guirec et de la Plage*. Open 25/3 – 5/11. 25 rooms.
Garden. Sea view. Tel: 96 91 40 89.

Plozévet 29710

** *Moulin de Brénizenec*. Open 30/10 – 25/9. 10 rooms.
Garden. Tel: 98 91 30 33.

Pont-Aven 29930

**** *Hotellerie de Keraven*. Open 1/4 – 15/11. 13 rooms. Sea view. Tel: 98 06 16 11.

** *Des Ajoncs d'Or*. Open all year. 24 rooms.
Tel: 98 06 02 06

Pont-l'Abbé 29120

** *Château de Kernuz*. Open 1/4 – 30/9. 18 rooms. Garden. Swimming-pool. Tel: 98 87 01 59

** *La Tour d'Auvergne*. Open all year. 27 rooms.
Tel: 98 87 00 47.

Pont-Scorff 56620

** *Le Fer à Cheval*. Open all year. 20 rooms. Garden.
Tel: 97 32 60 20.

Pontivy 56300

** *De l'Europe*. Open all year. 20 rooms. Garden. DB.
Tel: 97 25 11 14.

** *Du Porhoët*. Open all year. 28 rooms. Garden. DB.
Tel: 97 25 34 88.

** *Martin*. Open all year. 30 rooms. Tel: 97 25 02 04.

Pornic 44210

** *Beau Soleil*. Open all year. 15 rooms. Sea view.
Tel: 40 82 34 58.

** *Les Sablons*. Open all year. 30 rooms. Tennis. Garden. Sea view. Tel: 40 82 09 14

Port-Blanc 22710

** *Le Rocher*. Open 15/6 – 10/9. 10 rooms. Garden. Sea view. DB. Tel: 96 92 64 97.

Port-Louis 56290

** *Du Commerce*. Open all year. 40 rooms. Garden.
Tel: 97 82 46 05.

Pouldreuzic 29710

*** *Ker Ansquer*. Open 1/5 – 30/9. 11 rooms. Garden. Sea view. Tel: 98 54 41 83.

** *Breiz Armor*. Open 25/3 – 15/10. 23 rooms. Sea view. DB. Tel: 98 54 40 41.

Le Pouldu (Clohars-Carnoët) 29360

** *Des Bains*. Open 28/4 – 25/9. 49 rooms. Sea view. DB.

Tel: 98 39 90 11.

** *Des Dunes*. Open 8/5 – 14/9. 49 rooms. Tennis. Garden.
Sea view. Tel: 98 39 90 88.

Questembert 56230

*** *Le Bretagne*. Open 15/3 – 31/1. 6 rooms. Garden.
Tel: 97 26 11 12.

** *De la Gare*. Open all year. 10 rooms. Swimming-pool.
Garden. Tel: 97 26 11 47.

Quiberon 56170

**** *Sofitel Diététique*. Open 1/2 – 31/12. 78 rooms. Tennis.
Swimming-pool. Sea view. Tel: 97 50 20 00.

*** *Europa*. Open 25/3 – 2/10. 56 rooms. Swimming-pool.
Garden. Sea view. DB. Tel: 97 50 25 00.

*** *Résidence Orion*. Open all year. 65 rooms. Garden. DB.
Tel: 97 30 42 74.

** *Bellevue*. Open 15/3 – 6/11. 42 rooms. Swimming-pool.
Garden. Sea view. DB. Tel: 97 50 16 28.

** *De Ker Morvan*. Open 15/2 – 30/10. 29 rooms. Garden.
Tel: 97 30 44 74.

** *Des Druides*. Open 25/3 – 30/9. 30 rooms. Sea view. DB.
Tel: 97 50 14 74.

** *Hoche*. Open 1/2 – 10/10. 39 rooms. Swimming-pool.
Garden. Sea view. Tel: 97 50 07 73.

** *Ibis*. Open 1/2 – 2/1. 96 rooms. Swimming-pool.
Garden. DB. Tel: 97 30 47 72.

** *Roch-Priol*. Open 1/2 – 30/11. 50 rooms. Garden. DB.
Tel: 97 50 04 86.

Quimper 29000

*** *Le Griffon (131 Route de Bénodet)*. Open all year. 50
rooms. Swimming-pool. Garden. Tel: 98 90 33 33.

*** *Novotel (Rte de Bénodet)*. Open all year. 92 rooms.
Garden Pool. DB. Tel: 98 90 46 26.

** *La Tour d'Auvergne (13 Rue des Reguaires)*. Open all year.
43 rooms DB: Tel: 98 95 08 70.

** *Ibis (Rue Gustave Eiffel)*. Open all year. 72 rooms. DB.
Tel: 98 90 53 80.

** *Le Transvaal (57 Rue Jean Jaurès)* Open all year. 44 rooms. Tel: 98 90 09 91.

** *Moderne (21 Bis, Ave de la Gare)* Open all year. 62 rooms. Garden. DB. Tel: 98 90 31 71.

Quimperlé 29300

*** *De l'Ermitage.* Open all year. 28 rooms. Swimming-pool. Garden. DB. Tel: 98 96 04 66.

* *De l'Europe.* Open all year. 22 rooms. Tel: 98 96 00 02.

Redon 35600

** *De Bretagne.* Open all year. 20 rooms. Garden. Tel: 99 71 00 42.

** *La France.* Open all year. 20 rooms. Tel: 99 71 06 11.

Rennes 35000

*** *Altéa Parc du Colombier (1 Rue du Capitaine Maignan).* Open all year. 140 rooms. DB. Tel: 99 31 54 54.

*** *Du Guesclin Ibis (5 Place de la Gare).* Open all year. 68 rooms. DB. Tel: 99 31 47 47.

*** *Novotel Alma (Ave du Canada).* Open all year. 98 rooms. Swimming-pool. Garden. DB. Tel: 99 50 61 32.

** *Astrid (32 Ave Louis Barthou)* Open all year. 30 rooms. DB. Tel: 99 30 82 38.

** *Campanile (1 Rue de la Chalotais).* Open all year. 40 rooms. Garden. DB. Tel: 99 41 44 44.

** *Climat de France (Rue André Meynier).* Open all year. 42 rooms. Garden. DB. Tel: 99 54 12 03.

** *De Bretagne (7 Bis, Place de la Gare).* Open all year. 46 rooms. DB. Tel: 99 31 48 48.

** *De Nemours (5 Rue de Nemours).* Open all year. 26 rooms. DB. Tel: 99 78 26 26.

** *Ibis (Cesson-Sévigné) (Centre Hotelier la Perrière).* Open all year. 76 rooms. Garden. DB. Tel: 99 83 93 93.

La Roche-Bernard 56130

** *Auberge des Deux Magots.* Open all year. 15 rooms. Tel: 99 90 60 75.

** *De Bretagne.* Open Easter – 1/11. 15 rooms. Tel: 99 90 60 65.

Roscoff 29680

*** *Le Brittany*. Open 1/3 – 15/11. 19 rooms. Swimming-pool. Garden. Sea view. DB. Tel: 98 69 70 78.

*** *Le Gulf Stream*. Open 15/3 – 15/10. 32 rooms. Swimming-pool. Garden. Sea view. DB. Tel: 98 69 73 19.

*** *Régina*. Open 30/3 – 30/10. 50 rooms. Sea view. Garden. Tel: 98 61 23 55.

** *La Résidence*. Open all year. 32 rooms. Garden. DB. Tel: 98 69 74 85.

** *Le Triton*. Open 1/2 – 15/11. 45 rooms. Garden. DB. Tel: 98 61 24 44.

** *Les Alizes*. Open all year. 18 rooms. Sea view. DB. Tel: 98 69 72 22.

** *Chardons Bleus*. Open all year. 10 rooms. Tel: 98 69 72 03.

** *Les Tamaris*. Open 1/4 – 31/10. 27 rooms. Sea view. DB. Tel: 98 61 22 99.

** *Talabardon*. Open 10/3 – 15/11. 38 rooms. Sea view. Tel: 98 61 24 95.

Rosporden 29140

** *Bourhis*. Open all year. 27 rooms. DB. Tel: 98 59 23 89.

Sables-d'Or-les-Pins 22240

** *Au Bon Accueil*. Open Easter – 30/9. 39 rooms. DB. Tel: 96 41 42 19.

** *De Diane*. Open 18/3 – 1/10. 36 rooms. Garden. Sea view. DB. Tel: 96 41 42 07.

** *L'Abordage*. Open 19/3 – 1/10. 39 rooms. Sea view. DB. Tel: 96 41 51 11.

** *Les Ajoncs d'Or*. Open 1/5 – 30/9. 70 rooms. Garden. Sea view. DB. Tel: 96 41 42 12.

St-Brieuc 22000

*** *Le Griffon (Rue de Guernsey)*. Open 9/1 – 24/12. 45 rooms. Tennis. Garden. DB. Tel: 96 94 57 62.

** *Ker Izel (20 Rue du Gouët)*. Open all year. 22 rooms. Garden. Tel: 96 33 46 29.

** *Le Pignon Pointu (16 Rue J J Rousseau)*. Open all year. 17
rooms. Garden. Tel: 96 33 02 39

** *Mon Hotel (19 Rue Jean Métairie)*. Open all year. 46
rooms. Garden. DB. Tel: 96 33 01 21.

St-Cast-le-Guildo 22380

*** *Ar Vro*. Open 8/6 – 3/9. 47 rooms. Garden. Sea view.
Tel: 96 41 85 01.

** *Des Dunes*. Open 15/3 – 4/11. 27 rooms. Tennis. Garden.
Tel: 96 41 80 31.

** *Ker Louis*. Open 1/5–15/9. 28 rooms. Tennis. Garden.
Sea view. Tel: 96 41 80 77.

*** *Les Arcades*. Open Easter – 1/10. 32 rooms. Sea view.
Tel: 96 41 80 50.

St-Gildas-de-Rhuys 56730

* *Giquel*. Open 1/6 – 3/9. 29 rooms. Garden.
Tel: 97 45 23 12

St-Guénolé 29760

** *Le Sterenn*. Open Easter – 1/10. 16 rooms. Sea view.
Tel: 98 58 60 36.

St-Jacut-de-la-Mer 22750

** *Le Vieux Moulin*. Open Easter – 1/10. 29 rooms. Garden.
Sea view. DB. Tel: 96 27 71 02.

St-Malo 35400

*** *Grand de Thermes (100 Bd Hébert)*. Open 1/2 – 31/12.
101 rooms. Swimming-pool. Sea view. DB.
Tel: 99 56 02 56.

*** *Central (6 Grande Rue)*. Open all year. 46 rooms. DB.
Tel: 99 40 87 70.

*** *De la Digue (49 Chaussée du Sillon)*. Open 1/3 – 15/11.
53 rooms. Tel: 99 56 09 26.

*** *Mercure (2 Chaussée du Sillon)*. Open all year. 70 rooms.
Sea view. DB. Tel: 99 56 84 84.

*** *Résidence Orion (33 Rue George V)*. Open all year. 71
rooms. Garden. DB. Tel: 99 82 29 40.

** *Grand de Courtoisville (69 Bd. Hébert)*. Open 30/3 – 15/11.
51 rooms. Garden. Tel: 99 40 83 83.

** *Grotte aux Fées (36 Chaussée du Sillon)*. Open all year. 42 rooms. Sea view. DB. Tel: 99 56 83 30.

** *De France et Chateaubriand (Place Chateaubriand)*. Open all year. 85 rooms. Sea view. DB. Tel: 99 56 66 52.

** *De l'Univers (Place Chateaubriand)*. Open all year. 66 rooms. Tel: 99 40 89 52.

** *Ibis (Ave du Gén. de Gaulle)*. Open all year. 73 rooms. Garden. DB. Tel: 99 82 10 10.

** *Le Louvre (2 Rue des Marins)*. Open 1/3 – 20/11. 45 rooms. Tel: 99 40 86 62.

** *Le Rochebonne (15 Bd. Chateaubriand)*. Open all year. 38 rooms. DB. Tel: 99 56 01 72

** *Le Servannais (4 Rue Amiral Magon)* Open all year. 46 rooms. Tel: 99 81 45 50.

** *Mascotte (76 Chaussée du Sillon)*. Open all year. 88 rooms. Garden. Sea view. DB. Tel: 99 40 36 36.

** *Résidence Surcouf (15 Rue de la Plage)*. Open all year. 17 rooms. Garden. Sea view. Tel: 99 40 20 08.

St-Michel-en-Grève 22300

** *Plage*. Open all year. 38 rooms. Sea view. DB. Tel: 96 35 74 43.

St-Pierre-Quiberon 56510

*** *De la Plage*. Open 20/3 – 15/10. 49 rooms. Sea view. Tel: 97 30 92 10.

St-Pol-de-Léon 29250

* *De France*. Open all year. 26 rooms. Garden. Tel: 98 69 00 14.

St-Quay-Portrieux 22410

*** *Ker Moor*. Open all year. 28 rooms. Tennis. Garden. Sea view. DB. Tel: 96 70 52 22.

** *Le Gerbot d'Avoine*. Open all year. 26 rooms. Garden. Sea view. Tel: 96 70 40 09.

Ste-Anne-d'Auray 56400

** *De la Paix*. Open 1/3 – 15/10. 29 rooms. Tel: 97 57 65 08

** *Le Moderne*. Open all year. 37 rooms. DB.

Tel: 97 57 66 55.

** *Myriam*. Open Easter – 1/10. 30 rooms. Garden.

Tel: 97 57 70 44.

Ste-Anne-la-Palud 29550

**** *De la Plage*. Open 30/3 – 10/10. 30 rooms. Tennis.
Swimming-pool. Garden. Sea view. DB. Tel: 98 92 50 12.

* *Ste-Anne*. Open all year. 18 rooms. Garden.

Tel: 98 92 50 10

Sarzeau 56370

** *Du Port (St Jacques)*. Open all year. 8 rooms. Sea view.
DB. Tel: 97 41 93 51.

* *La Chaumière de la Mer*. Open Easter – 30/9. 15 rooms.
Garden. Sea view. Tel: 97 67 35 75.

Sizun 29450

* *Des Voyageurs*. Open all year. 16 rooms. Tel: 98 68 80 35

Le Tour-du-Parc 56370

*** *La Croix du Sud*. Open all year. 34 rooms. Tennis.
Garden. Swimming-pool. DB. Tel: 97 67 30 20.

Trébeurden 22560

*** *Ti Al Lannec*. Open 17/3 – 13/11. 22 rooms. Garden.
Sea view. Tel: 96 23 57 26.

*** *Manoir de Lan-Kerellec*. Open 15/4 – 15/11. 13 rooms.
Tennis. Garden. Sea view. DB. Tel: 96 23 50 09.

** *Family*. Open all year. 25 rooms. Garden. Sea view.
Tel: 96 23 50 31.

** *Ker an Nod*. Open Easter – 1/11. 21 rooms. Sea view.
Tel: 96 23 50 21.

Trégastel 22730

*** *Armoric*. Open 4/5 – 25/9. 50 rooms. Tennis. Garden.
Sea view. DB. Tel: 96 23 88 16.

*** *Belle Vue*. Open 25/3 – 30/9. 33 rooms. Garden. Sea
view. DB. Tel: 96 23 88 18.

** *De la Mer et de la Plage*. Open 31/5 – 30/9. 38 rooms. Sea
view. Tel: 96 23 88 03.

** *Des Bains*. Open all year. 30 rooms. Garden. Sea view.
Tel: 96 23 88 09.

Tréguier 22220

  ** *Kastell Dinec'h*. Open 15/3 – 31/12. 15 rooms.
Swimming-pool. Garden. DB. Tel: 96 92 49 39.

Trégunc 29910

  ** *Le Menhir*. Open 15/3 – 15/10. 28 rooms. Garden. DB.
Tel: 98 97 62 35.

La Trinité-sur-Mer 56470

  ** *Le Rouzic*. Open 15/12 – 15/11. 32 rooms. Sea view. DB.
Tel: 97 55 72 06.

  ** *Panorama (St-Philibert)*. Open 31/3 – 30/9. 25 rooms.
Garden.
Tel: 97 55 00 56.

Le Tronchet 35540

  *** *Hostellerie de L'Abbatiale*. Open 15/2 – 31/12. 76 rooms.
Tennis. Swimming-pool. Garden. DB. Tel: 99 58 93 21.

Le Val-André/Pléneuf 22370

  ** *Grand*. Open 30/4 – 11/11. 39 rooms. Sea view. DB.
Tel: 96 72 20 56.

  ** *De France et du Petit Prince*. Open 1/4 – 1/11. 55 rooms.
Garden. DB. Tel: 96 72 22 52.

  ** *Le Clémenceau*. Open all year. 23 rooms. Sea view. DB.
Tel: 96 72 23 70.

Vannes 56000

  *** *Aquarium (Le Parc du Golfe)*. Open all year. 48 rooms.
Garden. Sea view. DB. Tel: 97 40 44 52.

  *** *La Marebaudière (4 Rue A. Briand)*. Open 6/1 – 17/12.
41 rooms. Garden. DB. Tel: 97 47 34 29.

  *** *Inter Manche Océan (31 Rue du Lt. Colonel Maury)*. Open
all year. 42 rooms. DB. Tel: 97 47 26 46.

  ** *Climat de France (Z.C. Luscanen-Ploëren)*. Open all year.
42 rooms. Garden. DB. Tel: 97 40 91 91.

  ** *Ibis (Rue E. Jourdan)*. Open all year. 59 rooms. Garden.
Tel: 97 63 61 11.

  ** *Image Ste-Anne (8 Pl. de la Libération)*. Open all year. 32
rooms. Tel: 97 63 27 36.

Vitré 35500

**   ** *Du Château*. Open all year. 15 rooms. Tel: 99 74 58 59.
**   ** *La Grenouillère*. Open all year. 19 rooms. Garden. DB.
Tel: 99 75 34 52.
**   ** *Le Petit Billot*. Open all year. 23 rooms.
Tel: 99 75 02 10.
Le Vivier-sur-Mer 35960
**   ** *Hotel de Bretagne*. Open 15/3 – 15/11. 29 rooms. Sea
view. Tel: 99 48 91 74.

N.B. Although neighbouring La Baule, Pornic and Nantes are
no longer officially in Brittany, some hotels in these popular
locations have been included.

For general information on hotels see the section entitled
ACCOMMODATION.

LEISURE ACTIVITIES AND SPECIAL INTEREST HOLIDAYS

When in France further information may be obtained on
leisure activities from the local Tourist Office (*Syndicat
d'Initiative*). Alternatively write in advance to:
   Comité Régional du Tourisme,
   3,Rue d'Espagne,
   BP 4175,
   35041 Rennes Cedex.
   Tel: 99 50 11 15.
For special interest holidays contact the Loisirs Accueil, a
government-backed reservation service (often with English-
speaking staff) who offer a wide range of activity and sports
holidays – everything from cookery and pottery to riding and
canoeing. for addresses see listings TOURIST OFFICES and
LOISIRS ACCUEIL.

Many British tour operators also offer activity based holidays.
See listings TOUR OPERATORS.

Arts and Crafts/Courses

In Brittany, a region where traditions change very slowly, you can still find dozens of workshops where traditional crafts are carried on in the time-honoured way. For example, at a large centre just outside Breasparts on the Morlaix road, you can see the work of more than two hundred artists and craftsmen and buy their products and at Locronan you can watch weavers at work. Large and small museums throughout the area have exhibitions of rural crafts, and there is a strong movement towards preserving the rural way of life and encouraging the regrowth of traditional crafts. The Regional Tourist Office and Loisirs Accueil will send you information on a wide variety of courses (with or without accommodation) including book-binding, jewellery-making, pottery, weaving, wood- and stone-carving.

Birdwatching

Large colonies of sea birds can be seen around the coasts of Brittany. Birdwatching walks are organized throughout the year, particularly in the Morbihan region which has the largest concentration of sea birds along the French Atlantic coast. Bird sanctuaries at Belle-Ile, Cap-Fréhel, Cap-Sizun, Ile Grande, Pointe de Grouin, and Les Sept Iles.

Boating

There are 404 miles of navigable rivers and canals. Situated along the Nantes-Brest canal, the Blavet and the Aulne rivers are 20 firms hiring out small craft to luxury cruisers (2–12 berth). No special licence is needed and any car driver should be able to handle a canal cruiser. Always drive on the right. Locks are free but you are expected to help with the sluices. Bicycle hire is usually offered and is worth the extra expense. If you like the idea of canal cruising but don't want any of the work involved, you might consider a Hotel-Barge cruise.

Further information, waterway guides, brochures etc. may be
obtained from:

    Comité de Promotion Touristique des Canaux Bretons et
    Voies Navigables de l'Ouest,
    3 Rue des Portes-Mordelaises
    Rennes 35000.

Or contact regional Tourist Offices or Loisirs Accueil – see
listings.

Inclusive canal cruising holidays also through British
companies. See listings – TOUR OPERATORS.

There are pleasure cruises on all the major rivers, lakes and
bays. Sea trips to the string of islands that lie off the coast. See
listings – BOAT TRIPS.

Casinos

In many coastal resorts including Bénodet, Dinard, Perros-
Guirec, Quiberon, Pléneuf-Val-André, St-Cast, St-Malo and
St-Quay-Portrieux.

Cookery Courses

France is the land of *haute cuisine* so where better to learn the
secrets of the professionals and acquire the technique of
preparing seafood, feather-light pastry, superb sauces and
nouvelle cuisine. Details of courses are available from the
Regional Tourist Office and the Loisirs Accueil. See listings –
TOURIST OFFICES and LOISIRS ACCUEIL. Some
British tour operators offer holidays which feature cookery
courses. See listings – TOUR OPERATORS.

For a cookery course combined with French language studies
contact:–

    C.I.E.L.,
    Centre Cristian Morvan,
    BP 6,

St-Jouan-des-Guerrets 35430,
France.
Tel: 99 81 91 70.

Cycling

Most large towns have bicycle and moped hire and repair
shops (*marchand de vélos*) although it is advisable to carry a
range of spares as French sizes are different. Bicycles can also
be hired from many stations in Brittany. See listings –
BICYCLE HIRE. Hire, too, at youth hostels and campsites.
Cycle tracks must be used where marked – *piste cycliste
obligatoire*. Local Tourist Offices will supply maps with
planned itineraries following routes through the most
picturesque parts of the region or based on a particular theme
– e.g., châteaux, parish closes, megaliths and canals. There
are around 150 cycle clubs. For details of inclusive cycling
holidays staying in hostels and campsites contact the Loisirs
Accueil. See listings for addresses. The mild slopes, quiet roads
and marked paths make this region excellent for this type of
travel. Also very necessary on some of the islands where cars
are not allowed.

GETTING YOUR BICYCLE THERE
N.B. A bicycle for personal use is imported free into France
with little formality. However, it should be in good condition
and fitted with a reflector, lights and a bell. If newly
purchased take the receipt along with you.
By air: Bicycles travel as part of the baggage allowance but
check with individual airlines that they accept them.
By ferry: Most companies make no charge. Enquire when
booking.
By British Rail: Rules are constantly changing. Up-to-date
information from main line stations.
In France: Bicycles can travel free as accompanied luggage
(*baggage à main*) on French Railways (SNCF) but only at
certain times and on certain trains. Look out for the bicycle

sign on SNCF timetables. You must load and unload it yourself and the railways do not accept responsibility for cycles carried as hand-luggage, though at most stations you can take out insurance to cover the journey. Otherwise it may be sent as unaccompanied luggage. In which case take it to the *baggage consigné* office at the outward station, fill in the appropriate form and pay the fee. Be warned that it can take up to five days to arrive.

Several British tour operators arrange inclusive cycling holidays. See listings – TOUR OPERATORS. Detailed information on cycling in France, rallies etc. from:

> The Cyclist Touring Club,
> 69 Meadrow, Godalming,
> Surrey. GU7 3HS.
> Tel: 04868 7217.

For the latest information on rail/bike travel in France and bicycle hire contact:

> French Railways,
> 179 Piccadilly,
> London W1V 0BA.
> (Personal callers only.)
> Or contact any British Rail Travel Centre.

For an information booklet on cycling tours arranged in France and one hundred overnight hostels contact:

> ABRI,
> 9 Rue des Portes-Mordelaises,
> Rennes 35000.
> Tel: 99 31 59 44.

The above also offer 30% reduction on travel on French Railways.

Farm Visits/Stays

While on holiday it is possible to visit many working farms
and agricultural shows. Local Tourist Offices will have details
of these plus visiting times. Sometimes an appointment is
necessary. Cattle and dairy farms, stud farms, farms
specializing in fruit and vegetables, geese- and duck-rearing
farms, cider farms, cheese dairies and factories, oyster beds
etc. – all these can be visited. Inclusive holidays staying on a
farm can sometimes be arranged through the Loisirs Accueil.
See listings – TOURIST OFFICES and LOISIRS
ACCUEIL. Or write for details of farm holidays to:

Agriculture et Tourisme,
9 Avenue George V,
Paris 75008.

Fishing

Brittany boasts 6,000 miles of well-stocked rivers and canals
but a permit is required (*permit de pêche*). This is easily
available – enquire at the local Tourist Office. Rivers are
divided into two categories – 1st category (*première catégorie*) is
predominantly trout and salmon and 2nd category (*deuxième
catégorie*) is practically everything else. There are special
regulations relating to salmon (*saumon*) and trout (*truite*). Get
advice with permit. Do not fish in waters marked '*clos*' as
these are private although the owner may give permission if
asked. Never fish in nature parks and reserves.

Hundreds of miles of coastline provide ideal conditions for
catching crab and cockling. No special permit is required for
amateur sea-fishers but regulations state that you must not
have more than twelve hooks on conventional lines or more
than thirty hooks suspended by floats.

There are also clubs for spear-fishing.

Regional information centre for river fishing:–

La Maison de la Rivière,
de l'Eau et de la Pêche
Moulin de Vergraon,
Sizun 29450.

For sea fishing:

Fédération de Pêche en Mer,
Pont Roux, Le Yaudet,
Ploumilliau,
Lannion 22300.

Golfing

Brittany is considered by many to be the foremost golfing
region in France with its rich green countryside not unlike
parts of Scotland. It has many well maintained nine- and
eighteen-hole golf courses with very reasonable charges. See
listings – GOLF COURSES.

Daily and weekly rates, also special rates for couples (ask for
ménage). Discounts of up to 15% on green fees are often
available where booked through a specialist tour operator,
who can also arrange a whole package travelling with your
own car or fly/drive. See listings – TOUR OPERATORS.

Some golf courses are attached to luxury hotels who offer
saunas, swimming-pools, tennis courts and other sporting
facilities. Most clubs run weekend competitions in which
visitors may usually participate so serious golfers are advised
to take handicap certificates with them. N.B. Golf balls are
expensive so take your own with you.

Group Travel/Activities

The best people to approach for making group reservations
are the Loisirs Accueil booking offices who also specialize in

arranging sports/activity/special interest holidays for groups.
See listings TOURIST OFFICES and LOISIRS ACCUEIL.
They can arrange accommodation, (hotels, campsites, hostels)
hire of coaches, boats etc. Most UK tour operators can
accommodate group bookings and indeed sometimes give a
discount for large parties. Several specialize in group travel
tailoring the holiday to suit the particular interest of your
school, club, society or party. See listings – TOUR
OPERATORS.

Language Courses

Several British Companies organize language courses in
private schools and universities catering for all ages and
abilities with accommodation in hotels, halls of residence and
private homes. Some of these holidays combine a traditional
villa or hotel holiday with classes for only a few hours a day,
the rest of the time being free to do your own thing. This is a
good option for families where all the members do not wish to
join the language lessons. See listings – TOUR
OPERATORS. Most courses are in fact combined with other
leisure and sports activities and sightseeing.

Other organizations which will arrange language courses in
France, again with accommodation, are:

The Central Bureau,
Seymour Mews House,
Seymour Mews, London W1H 9PE.
Tel: 071 486 5101.

and at
3, Bruntsfield Crescent,
Edinburgh. EH10 4HD.
Tel: 031 447 8024

16, Malone Road,
Belfast. BT9 5BN.
Tel: 0232 664418/9.

The French Centre,
61–69 Chepstow Place,
London W2 4TR.
Tel: 071 221 8134.

Alternatively write direct to any of the following in France
requesting information on their summer French Language
courses:

Cours d'Eté de Quimper
Faculté des Lettres,
BP 860,
Brest Cedex 29200, France.

Cours Universitaire d'Eté,
BP 125,
St-Malo Cedex 35402, France.

C.I.E.L.,
Centre Christian Morvan,
BP 6,
St-Jouan-des-Guerrets 35430,
France.

and young people only –

Accueil des Jeunes en France,
12 Rue des Barrés,
Paris 75004.

Motoring

Apart from weekends at the height of the season traffic is
generally light. Quiet country roads cutting through the
varied terrain of lush countryside, forests, moors and coastal
cliff tops make this a delightful area for motoring. For single
base self-drive or 'go as you please' – type holidays there is a
wide range of accommodation available. If taking your own
car you might make use of an advance booking service to

reserve accommodation (one or more nights) in hotels, B & B's, apartments, *gîtes* and even tents. Advance reservations can also be made on campsites for your own tent or caravan. All these types of holidays can be booked through British tour operators. See listings – TOUR OPERATORS.

If you intend hiring a car in France there are plenty of agencies there but you will probably get a better deal by booking a fly-drive holiday though an Airline Company or tour operator. French Railway (SNCF) also offer very competitive rates.

In Brittany local Tourist Offices will supply maps and motoring routes for sightseeing.

Riding

Over 2,000 miles of bridlepaths and 30 riding centres. Some offer accommodations in *gîtes*. For lists of riding schools, itineraries and useful addresses contact:

Association Régionale du Tourisme Equestre en Bretagne
8 Rue de la Carrière,
Josselin 56120.
Tel: 97 22 22 62.

When in France local Tourist Offices will be able to provide information on riding schools, rates etc. Inclusive riding holidays can be booked through a Loisurs Accueil office. See listings – TOURIST OFFICES and LOISIRS ACCUEIL.

For an alternative and extremely pleasant way of seeing Brittany, horse-drawn caravans (*roulottes*) may be hired for weekends or by the week from –

Roulottes de Bretagne,
Gare de Locmaria-Berrien,
Le Huelgoat 29690.
Tel: 98 99 73 28.
(Finistère)

Roulottes du Sud-Cornouaille,
Porz an Breton,
Quimperlé 29300.
Tel: 98 96 16 56.
(Finistère)

Cheval Langon Loisirs,
Langon 35660.
Tel: 99 08 76 42.
(Ille-et-Vilaine)

Attelages Morbihannais,
Ker Samuel,
Le Saint 56610.
Tel: 97 23 06 16
(Morbihan)

Sea-Water Health Treatments

There are nine marine hydrotherapy institutions where you
can combine a seaside holiday in luxury surroundings with a
planned programme which makes the most of the health-
giving properties of sea-water and sea-air. See listings – SEA
WATER TREATMENT CENTRES.

Short Breaks

Being within easy reach of the UK Brittany is an ideal region
for enjoying a taste of France – its wonderful food and wine,
dramatic coastline, beautiful countryside, medieval towns and
villages, châteaux and splendid Gothic cathedrals. Short
breaks are anything from one to five nights and
accommodation ranges from *gîtes*, country and seaside inns to
five-star and châteaux hotels where the emphasis is on luxury
and gastronomic delights. For UK Companies offering these
see listings – TOUR OPERATORS.

Sightseeing

The visitor to Brittany will find a rich architectural heritage of medieval towns, walled cities, Gothic cathedrals, parish closes and sculptured calvaries not to mention its world-famous prehistoric sites and areas of great natural beauty. Fortified castles form a line across Brittany's eastern frontier, many of them set among woods and splendid gardens. Lovers of fine art will want to visit the galleries at Pont-Aven where Gauguin established a school in 1880 and at Quimper where they have a fine collection of Impressionist paintings.

Excursions by coach leave from all the larger towns and there are boat trips along the inland waterways, to the islands, bird sanctuaries and around the bays.

The following lighthouses are open to the public: Bénodet, Cap Fréhel, Le Conquet, Ile-de-Batz, Ile-de-Sein, Ouessant Island, Penmarc'h, Plouarzel, Plougonvelin, Plouguerneau, Plouzane, Roscoff (all in Finistère) and Bangor (Morbihan). Contact the local Tourist Office and make an appointment with the keeper.

Most towns have at least one museum specializing in anything from ancient shoes, musical instruments and artifacts to military uniforms, dolls and vintage cars. Full details of all the above, plus parks, zoos, aquaria and lighthouses to visit can be found in the listings under the appropriate heading. Local Tourist Offices will be happy to provide information on what to see and do and to supply maps, routes, itineraries, etc.

Walking and Rambling

Increasingly popular holiday activity in Brittany which has over 2,500 miles of blazed footpaths with hostels and

reasonable accommodation along the routes. All way-marked
trails are colour coded as follows:

Grandes Randonnées (long-distance and inter-regional trails)
are marked with red and white horizontal slashes.

Sentiers de Pays (local trails) usually marked in red and
yellow. Trail numbers and colours are shown on trees, rocks,
boards or posts.

Grandes Randonnées trails in Brittany include:

GR37. Between Sillé-le-Guillaume and Huelgoat via Vitré,
Dinan and Josselin.

GR34. Between Huelgoat and Douarnenez.

GR341. Between St-Brieuc and Paimpol via the coast.

GR347. Between Josselin and Redon.

GR39. Between Rennes and Mont-St-Michel.

GR380. Between Morlaix and Huelgoat. (Takes in the three
most famous parish closes.)

For further information on walking and cycling including one
hundred overnight hostels contact:

Abri, La Maison de la Randonnée,
9 Rue des Portes-Mordelaises,
Rennes 35000.
Tel: 99 31 59 44.

Information also from Tourist Offices who can supply maps
which also show places of interest, restaurants and bars.
Inclusive walking holidays available through Loisirs Accueil
offices and tour operators. See appropriate listings.

Maps and guides to the GR footpaths can be obtained in
good bookshops in France. In London:

Stanfords Travel Guide Bookshop,
12, Long Acre,
London WC2E 9LP.
Tel: 071 836 1321.

Water Sports

With good beaches dotted all along the seven hundred miles of coastline, swimming and all other water sports are extremely popular. Realizing, however, that these can be dangerous, the French have set up a lifeguard system with stations at all the major resorts – helicopters, etc., so it is advisable to swim and practise any aquatic sports at one of these. Different coloured flags are used to indicate degree of safety: green for safe, orange for dangerous and red for swimming prohibited.

Brittany, often called the yachtsman's paradise, has over thirty superb marinas around the coast plus numerous spots where mooring is permitted. Also dozens of sailing schools including the famous international one on the Iles de Glenans. In fact most resorts have their own yachting or windsurfing schools open to all. There are frequent yachting regattas and competitions. For a list of yachting schools or other sailing information write to:

Comité Régional du Tourisme de Bretagne,
3 Rue d'Espagne,
BP 4175, 35041 Rennes Cedex.

La Ligue Haute-Bretagne,
1 Rue des Fours à Chaux,
Cancale 35260.
(For Ille-et-Vilaine and Côtes-Du-Nord departments).
La Ligue d'Armour, 2 Cours de la Bôve,
Lorient 56100.
(For Morbihan and Finistère).
Excellent facilities all over for windsurfing, sailboarding, canoeing, scuba diving, motorboating and water-skiing.

For regulations and other information relating to under water diving and spear fishing write to:

Comité Régional Bretagne-Normandie de la Fédération
Française d'Etude des Sports Sous-marins,
78 Rue Ferdinand,
Buisson, St-Nazaire 44600.

Youth Travel

Several British tour operators specialize in holidays for young
people, school travel, sports and adventure-type holidays. See
listings – TOUR OPERATORS.

Two other organizations are worth mentioning here:

The French Centre,
61–69 Chepstow Place, London
W2 4TR. Tel: 071 221 8134.

They can help find reasonably priced accommodation in
hotels, campsites, universities, youth centres and with families.
They also arrange language and other courses with all kinds
of activity holidays for both individuals and groups and, with
their own hostel accommodation in London, may be able to
accommodate you en route for France.

The second organization is –

The Central Bureau,
Seymour Mews House, Seymour Mews,
London W1H 9PE.
Tel: 071 486 5101.
(Also at 3, Bruntsfield Cres.
Edinburgh, EH10 4HD.
Tel: 031 447 8024
and 16 Malone Road, Belfast. BT9 5BN. Tel: 0232 664418/
9).

The above provide information and advice on all forms of
educational exchanges and visits including: French language
courses in France; teacher exchange schemes; putting schools

in touch with partners in France; organizing pen pals for the 10 to 18 age group; student and young worker placings and exchanges.

Their publications include the following:
Working Holidays – information on hundreds of paid and voluntary work opportunities.
Volunteer Work – information on organizations and agencies.
Home for Home – a guide to home stays and exchange visits.

The Student Travel Conference publish *The Sleep Cheap Guide* which provides a list of hotel, *pension* and hostel accommodation in France. It is available from most student travel offices.

Young people under twenty-six holding a valid Youth International Education Exchange card and full-time students up to the age of thirty can book reduced rate air, rail and ferry travel through any Student Travel Office, appointed USIT agent or direct at USIT, 52, Grosvenor Gardens, London SW1. Tel: 071 730 7285.

For Youth Hostels in Brittany contact:
   Association Bretonne des Auberges de Jeunesse,
   La Haute-Boë,
   Fleurigne 35133.
or contact
   The Youth Hostels Association,
   14 Southampton Street,
   London WC2. Tel: 071 836 1036 for their International Handbook.
See also listings – YOUTH HOSTELS.

MEGALITHIC MONUMENTS

Brittany is particularly rich in these relics of prehistoric times. They fall into the following categories:

Menhirs

Upright standing stones thought to be symbols of eternity.
These are usually found in rectangular or circular patterns.
Famous collections are those at Er Lannic on a tiny island on
the Golfe du Morbihan, Carnac where there are 3,000 and
Erdeven which has over 1,100 all in Morbihan. Large
collection at St-Just (Ille-et-Vilaine), and Lagat-Jar at
Camaret-sur-Mer (Finistère) which has 143.

Dolmens

Round or rectangular funeral chambers found in the
Departments of Finistère and Morbihan. One of the most
famous is to be found at Locmariaquer.

Roofed Passages

Galleries in the form of elongated rectangles sometimes
divided into several chambers. The best known are at Roche
aux Fées (Ille-et-Vilaine) and at Commana (Finistère).

Cairns

Dolmens were enclosed in either dry-stone structures known
as cairns or in earth tumuli. The most interesting is to be
found at Plouezoc'h (Finistère) and contains eleven funeral
chambers and passages.

MONASTERIES OFFERING ACCOMMODATION

Abbaye La Joie Notre-Dame
(Cistercian),
Campénéac,
Ploërmel 56800.
(Morbihan)
Abbaye Notre-Dame de Timadeuc

(Cistercian),
Rohan 56580.
(Morbihan)
Abbaye Saint-Guénolé
(Benedictine),
Landevennec
Plomodiern 29550.
(Finistère)
Abbaye Saint-Michel de Kergonan
(Benedictine),
Plouharnel 56720.
(Morbihan)
Abbaye Saint-Anne de Kergonan
(Benedictine),
Plouharnel 56720.
(Morbihan)
Monastère Notre-Dame de Beaufort
(Benedictine),
Plerguer,
Miniac-Morvan 35540.
(Ille-et-Vilaine)

MUSEUMS AND EXHIBITIONS

(Consult local Tourist Offices for Opening and Closing
Times).

COTES-DU-NORD

Binic
Local History and Marine Museum.
Corseul
Archaeological Museum.
Dinan
Duchess Anne's Castle Museum.

Bird Museum.
La Chèze
Handicraft and Breton Culture Museum.
Lamballe
Mathurin Meheut Museum (Breton Painter).
Old Lamballe Museum of Folk Art.
Paimpol
Maritime Museum.
Floating Museum 'Mad Atao' (Ship with old rigging classified as historical monument).
Plédéliac
Saint-Esprit-des-Bois Farm (Reconstruction of early 20th-century farm).
Plédran
Archaeological Site of Saint-Péran.
Pleudihen-sur-Rance
Apple and Cider Museum.
Pleumeur-Bodou
Ile Grande Bird Sanctuary and Exhibition.
Trégor Planetarium.
Saint-Brieuc
Local History Museum.
Trégastel
Marine and Prehistoric Museum.
Tréguier
Renan Museum (House of the famous philosopher).

FINISTERE

Audierne
La Chaumière Museum (Breton interiors and furniture).
Pointe-du-Raz Museum (Reproductions of Breton calvaries).
Brest
Municipal Museum.
Art Museum (Pont-Aven school).
Brest Castle Maritime Museum.

Motte-Tanguy Tower Museum (Local history museum).
Camaret
Naval Museum.
Commana
Ecomuseum of Monts d'Arrée (Reconstruction of village life).
Concarneau
Fishing Museum.
Marine Museum.
Combrit
Music Museum.
Douarnenez
Boat Museum.
Locronan
Folk Art Museum.
Loctudy
Kerazan Museum (Old house with paintings/furnishings).
Morlaix
Jacobins Museum (Local history, paintings, furniture and sculpture).
Ouessant Island
Ecomuseum (18th-century house with furniture, utensils, *objets d'art*).
Plougeurneau
Maritime Museum.
Pont-l'Abbé
Bigouden Museum (Local history, clothes, arts and crafts).
Pays Bigouden House (Reconstruction of early 20th-century farm).
Pont-Aven
Pont-Aven Art Museum.
Quimper
Fine Art Museum.
Max Jacob Art Museum.
Pottery Museum.
Local History Museum.
Quimperlé

'Maison des Archers' (Traditional museum in 15th-century manor house).

Saint-Guénolé-Penmarc'h
Prehistoric Museum.
Saint-Rivoal
'La Maison Cornec' Museum (Local history/traditions).
Saint-Thurien
Kerchuz Mill Museum (Old mill - milling techniques).
Saint-Vouguay
Château de Kerjean Museum (Breton furniture and art).
Trégarvan
Rural School Museum.

ILLE-ET-VILAINE

Baguer-Morvan
Agricultural Museum.
Cancale
Local History Museum.
Dinard
Dinard Museum.
Dol-de-Bretagne
History Museum.
Fougères
Shoe Museum.
De La Villéon Art Museum.
Monfort-sur-Meu
Folk Museum.
Paimpont
Abbey Museum.
Québriac
Fauna Museum.
Rennes
Museum of Brittany.
Rennes (Cesson-Sévigné)
Automobile Museum.

Saint-Malo
Cap-Hornier Museum (Maritime museum).
Castle Museum (Local history).
Jacques Cartier Manor House Museum (Life and travels of J. Cartier who discovered Canada).
Quic-En-Groigne Museum (Waxworks).
Doll Museum.
Tinténiac
Handicraft Museum.

MORBIHAN

Baden
Old Toy Museum.
Belle-Ile-en-Mer (Le-Palais)
Citadel Museum (Local history).
Bignan
Centre for Local Contemporary Art.
Brech (Auray)
Local History Museum.
Carnac
Miln Le Rouzic Museum (Prehistoric).
Chapelle-Caro
Crevys Castle Museum (Uniforms).
Guer
Saint-Cyr-Coetquidan Military Museum.
Groix
Local History Museum.
Inzinzc-Lochrist
Ethnographic Museum of the Hennebont Forges (Local history).
Josselin
Doll Museum.
Lorient
East India Company Museum.
Marine Museum.

Peillac
Local History Museum.
Port-Louis
Citadel Atlantic Museum (Maritime museum).
Quistinic
Museum of Local Arts and Traditions.
Rochefort-en-Terre
History Museum.
Sainte-Anne-d'Auray
Sacred Art Museum.
History Museum.
Saint-Marcel
Museum of the Resistance Movement.
Vannes
Gaillard Castle Museum (Prehistoric).

N.B. Admission charges vary but many, especially the larger museums, have one free day, usually Wednesdays or Sundays. Check if there are reductions for children, students, disabled and senior citizens.

NATURIST CLUBS AND CAMPSITES

Koad Ar Roc'h
(Monsieur A. Bossard),
Château du Bois de la Roche,
Néant-sur-Yvel 56820.
Tel: 97 74 42 11.
Large naturist holiday centre and campsite in south-east Brittany (15 km from Ploëmel) set among a vast area of meadows and woods overlooked by a medieval castle. It has a working farm, clubhouse, shop, bar, and restaurant. Swimming and boating on lakes. Riding and fishing. Bungalows to rent. Craft centre in the village. Open all year.

Les Bruyères d'Arvor
Cléguer,
Lorient 56100.
Small campsite 17 km north of Lorient. Set in quiet wood-
land with club house. Shopping in nearby village. Open mid-
June to mid-September.

NATURIST BEACHES

Although officially no authorized naturist beaches, nude
bathing and sunbathing are tolerated at some. For up-to-date
information on these and naturist holiday centres throughout
France contact:

> The Central Council for British Naturism,
> Assurance House,
> 35–41 Hazelwood Road,
> Northampton. NN1 1LL.
> Tel: 0604 20361.

For a full colour brochure on French Naturist Holiday
Centres write to:

> Fédération Française de Naturisme,
> 53 Rue de la Chaussée,
> D'Antin,
> Paris 75009.

> Request English edition (free) and enclose International
> Reply Coupon.

PARDONS AND FESTIVALS

The *pardon* is a religious festival during which the participants
ask forgiveness for their sins. It is an important feature of
Breton life and culture and takes place in towns and villages
throughout the summer. The religious ceremony is almost

always followed by more lively celebrations involving Breton music played on ancient instruments and folk dancing. Traditional costumes are worn, the women in heavily embroidered dresses and superb lace headdresses, the men in be-ribboned hats and breeches and the children decked out in their own miniature versions. The greatest *pardons*, such as those of Sainte-Anne-La-Palud and Sainte-Anne-d'Auray, and the most colourful and spectacular festivals, such as those held at Quimper, Lorient and Concarneau, attract tens of thousands of visitors from France and abroad.

MAIN PARDONS

COTES-DU-NORD

Bulat Pestivien
2nd Sunday in September.
Guingamp
1st Sunday in July.
Kérity-Paimpol
28 May.
Perros-Guirec
15 August.
Plouha
3rd Sunday in September.
Quintin
2nd Sunday in May.
Saint-Brieuc
Last weekend in May.
Saint-Quay-Portrieux
End of July.
Tréguier
End of May.
Le Vieux-Marché
End of July.

FINISTERE

Douarnenez/Sainte-Anne-la-Palud
Last Sunday in August.
Le Folgoët
1st Sunday in September.
Locronan
2nd Sunday in July.
Pont-Croix
15 August.
Rumengol
Sunday after Pentecost.
15 August
Saint-Guénolé-Penmarc'h
15 August.
Saint-Jean-Trolimon
3rd Sunday in September.
Trégunc
Last Sunday in August.

MORBIHAN

Belz
3rd Sunday in September.
Carnac
2nd Sunday in September.
Le Faouët
End of June.
Last Sunday in August.
Guénin
End of July.
Josselin
2nd Sunday in September.
Pontivy
3rd Sunday in September.
Rochefort-en-Terre
Sunday after 15 August.

Sainte-Anne-d'Auray
25 and 26 July.
La Trinité-Porhoët
Pentecost.

MAIN FESTIVALS

COTES-DU-NORD

Dinan
International Music Festival in July.
Fréhel
Festival in July.
Guingamp
Breton Dance Festival in mid-August.
Lamballe
Folk Festival. 2nd Sunday in July.
Paimpol
Festival in mid-July.
Perros-Guirec
Flower Festival. 16 August.
Pleubian
Festival in July.
Ploëzal-Runan
Cultural Festivals and events between May and September.
Saint-Brieuc
Breton May Festival.
Music Festival in early July.

FINISTERE

Beuzec-Cap-Sizun
Heather Festival. 2nd Sunday in August.
Châteauneuf-du-Faou
International Dance and Traditions Festival. 15 August.
Concarneau
Blue Nets Festival. 3rd Sunday in August.

Fouesnant
Apple Festival. 3rd Sunday in July.
Morlaix
Wednesday Festivals. July–August.
Plomodiern
Menez-Hom Festival. 15 August.
Plozévet
International Folklore Festival in mid-July.
Pont-Aven
Yellow Gorse Festival. 1st Sunday in August.
Pont-l'Abbé
Embroidery Festival. 2nd Sunday in July.
Quimper
International Folk Festival during 2nd fortnight in July.
Quimperlé
Festival at Pentecost.

ILLE-ET-VILAINE

Bécherel
Festival in July.
Dinard
International Music and Dance Festivals in August.
Fougères
Summer drama festival. Late August/early September.
Hédé
Festival in mid-August.
Monterfil
Music Festival and Competition in mid-June.
Redon
Abbey Festival. Mid-July – mid-August.
Rennes
Arts Festival. End June/early July.
Saint-Briac
Festival of the Seagull. 2 August.
Saint-Malo

Festival in July.
Festival of Sacred Music at the beginning of August.
Vivier-sur-Mer
Festival in July.

MORBIHAN

Auray
International Festival of Music and Dance in mid-July.
Carnac
Standing Stone Festival. 3rd Sunday in August.
Lizio
Craft Festival in mid-August.
Lorient
Theatre Festival. 2nd fortnight in July.
International Celtic Festival. 1st fortnight in August.
Suscinio
Arts Festival. 5 – 18 August.
Vannes
Arvor Festival. 15 August.

PARKS AND GARDENS

(For times of opening and further information contact local
Tourist Offices)

Many châteaux and abbeys have attractive gardens and one
continually comes across small villages which have been given
the official title of *Village Fleuri* because of their marvellous
floral displays. There are also some large gardens open to the
public including the following:

FINISTERE

Brest
Botanical gardens in the Stanglarc'h valley.

Collection of rare plants and magnificent public garden.

Combrit
Jardin Botanique de Cornouaille
Thousands of different species, aquatic plants, rose gardens, etc.

Saint-Goazec/Châteauneuf-du-Faou
Parc de Trévarez
One of Europe's loveliest parks in the heart of the Black Mountains. Château, park, nurseries and woods.

ILLE-ET-VILAINE

Rennes
Le Thabor Parcs et Jardins
Landscaped park with large variety of species.

MORBIHAN

Bignan
Domaine de Kerguéhennec
Large park with woods, lawns and lake surrounding 18th-century castle. Also setting for National Arts Centre.

Hennebont
Parc de Kerbihan
Botanical garden with plant species from all over the world.

NATIONAL PARKS

FINISTERE

Parc d'Armorique
This vast nature and conservation park covers 170,000 acres of rugged countryside and heather-clad hills. Within its boundaries lie thirty towns and villages, many with interesting churches, Breton museums and craftshops. At the

coast there are breathtaking views from the cliff tops. Visitors are welcomed to the park at the *Maison d'Accueil*, Hanvec.

SEA-WATER TREATMENT (THALASSOTHERAPY) CENTRES

The following centres offer treatments based on the health-giving qualities of sea-water, seaweed and sea-air all under medical supervision. Apart from hydrotherapy, other treatments include physiotherapy and massage. Medical conditions treated range from backache and asthma to rheumatism and sinusitis. Those seeking slimming cures, relief from stress and convalescents are also catered for. Treatments are offered on a daily or weekly basis.

Apart from the medical regimes, these centres normally offer a range of leisure and sports activities and excursions.

COTES-DU NORD

Institut de Thalassothérapie,
Grand Hotel,
Plage de Trestraou,
Perros-Guirec 22700.
Tel: 96 23 28 97.
Open February to November.

FINISTERE

Centre des Néréides,
Thermes Marins,
Corniche de la Plage,
Bénodet 29950.
Tel: 98 57 20 62.
Open May to September.

Centre Ker An Nod,
Bénodet 29950.
Tel: 98 57 02 55.

Centre de Cure Marine de la Baie de Tréboul,
BP 4,
Rue Pierre Curie,
Douarnenez 29100.
Tel: 98 92 30 50.
Open all year.

Institut Centre Ker Lena,
BP 13, Roscoff 29680.
Tel: 98 61 24 15
or 98 69 70 31.
Open all year.

Institut Centre de Thalassothérapie-Rockroum,
BP 28, 29680
Roscoff.
Tel: 98 69 72 15.
Open April to October.

ILLE-ET-VILAINE

Les Thermes Marins,
Grande Plage,
100 Boulevard Hebert,
BP 32,
Saint-Malo 35401.
Tel: 99 56 02 56.
Open February to December.

MORBIHAN

Centre de Thalassothérapie,
BP 83, Carnac 56340.
Tel: 97 52 04 44.
Open January to November.

Institut de Thalassothérapie,
BP 170, Quiberon 56170.
Tel: 97 50 20 00.
Open February to December.

For further information, leaflets etc. contact:
The Regional Tourist Office,
CRT,
3, Rue d'Espagne,
BP 4175,
35041 Rennes Cedex.
Tel: 99 50 11 15.

TOUR OPERATORS (British) and types of holidays offered.

AA Motoring Holidays
PO Box 100, Fanum House,
Halesowen, B63 3BT.
Tel: 021 550 7401.
Villas, apartments, mobile homes and motoring.

A.L.I.S. Holidays
92 Upper Village Road, Sunninghill,
Ascot, SL5 7AQ.
Tel: 0344 23204.
French courses for children (escorted).

Agricultural Travel Bureau
14 Chain Lane, Newark, NG 24 1AU.
Tel: 0636 705612.
Agricultural/horticultural tours

Air France Holidays
69 Boston Manor Road,
Brentford, Middx, TW8 9JQ.
Tel: 081 568 6981.
Fly/drive and short-break holidays.

All-Association for Active Learning
9 Haywra Street, Harrogate, HG1 5BJ.
Tel: 0423 505313.

Mobile-home holidays. Sea fishing/boating holidays.
Language courses.

Allez France

27 West Street, Storrington,

West Sussex, RH20 4DZ.

Tel: 0903 745793.

Gîte, villa and hotel holidays. Also holiday villages.

Angel Travel

34 High Street,

Borough Green, Kent, TN15 8BJ.

Tel: 0732 884109.

Villas, *gîtes* and apartment holidays.

Auto-plan Holidays

2nd Floor Suite, Energy House,

Lombard Street, Lichfield, WS13 6DP.

Tel: 0543 257777.

Villas, country houses, apartment and hotel holidays.

Avon Europe

Lower Quinton, Stratford-upon-Avon,

Warwickshire, CV37 8SG.

Tel: 0789 720130.

Gîte and villa holidays.

B & B Abroad

5 World's End Lane, Green Street

Green, Orpington, Kent, BR6 6AA.

Tel: 0689 55538.

Overnight stops and short breaks in private B & B
accommodation.

Beach Villas

8 Market Passage, Cambridge, CB2 3QR.

Tel: 0223 311113.

Villa and apartment holidays.

Bebb Travel

The Coach Station,

Llantwit Fardre, Pontypridd, CF38 2HB

Tel: 0443 204211.

Coach holidays
Becks Holidays
Southfields, Shirleys, Ditchling,
West Sussex, BN6 8UD.
Tel: 07918 2843.
Mobile-home holidays.
Billington Travel
2a White Hart Parade,
Riverhead, Sevenoaks, TN13 2BJ.
Tel: 0732 460666.
Hotel, *gîte* and motoring holidays
Blakes Holidays
Wroxham, Norwich, NR12 8DH.
Tel: 0603 784131.
Villas and country houses. River and canal cruising.
Blue Line Cruisers
PO Box 9, Hayling Island, PO11 0NL.
Tel: 0705 466111.
Canal Cruising.
Bob-A-Long
Harbour Road, Rye, TN31 7TE.
Tel: 0797 226770.
Walking holidays.
Bowhills
Mayhill Farm, Mayhill Lane,
Swanmore, Southampton, SO3 2RD.
Tel: 0489 877627.
Farmhouses, *gîtes* and villas.
Branta Travel
11 Uxbridge Street, London W8 7TQ.
Tel: 071 229 7231.
Birdwatching holidays
Breakaway Holidays
14 West Street, Storrington,
West Sussex, RH20 4EE.
Tel: 0903 742366.

Mobile-home holidays.

Brittany Caravan Hire
15 Winchcombe Road,
Frampton Cotterell, Bristol, BS17 2AG.
Tel: 0454 772410.
Camping, caravanning, villas, *gîtes*, apartments and
holiday villages.

Brittany Direct Holidays
362 Sutton Common Road, Sutton, Surrey, SM3 9PL.
Tel: 081 641 6060.
Gîtes, villas and apartments. Hotel, *chambre d'hôtes* and
golfing holidays.

Brittany Ferries
The Brittany Centre, Wharf Road,
Portsmouth, PO2 8RU.
Tel: 0705 751708 or 0705 751833.
Gîtes, apartments, châteaux, hotels, camping/caravanning.
Short breaks, motoring, canal cruising and golfing

Brittany Villas
Holiday House, 2 Monson Road,
Tunbridge Wells, TN1 1NN.
Tel: 0892 36616.
Villa and cottage holidays.

Cafe Couette
PO Box 66, 94 Bell Street,
Henley on Thames, RG9 1XS.
Tel: 0491 578803.
Bed and breakfast in private homes.

Camping Service
69 Westbourne Grove, London W2 4UJ.
Tel: 071 792 1944.
Campsite booking service.

Canvas Holidays
Bull Plain, Hertford, Herts, SG14 1DY.
Tel: 0992 553535.
Tent and mobile home holidays. Bird-watching holidays.

Car Holidays Abroad

Contact Canvas Holidays as above.

Carasol Holidays

6 Hayes Avenue,

Bournemouth, BH7 7AD.

Tel: 0202 33398

Mobile-homes. Villa and apartment holidays.

Carefree Camping

126 Hempstead Road, Kings Langley,

Herts, WD4 8AL.

Tel: 09277 61311.

Tent and mobile-home holidays.

Carisma Holidays

Bethel House, Heronsgate Road,

Chorleywood, Herts, WD3 5BB.

Tel: 09278 4235.

Mobile-home holidays.

Chalets de France

Travel House, Pandy,

Nr. Abergavenny, NP7 8DH.

Tel: 0873 890770.

Chalet and mobile-home holidays.

Chez Nous

Netherley House, 85 Dobb Top Road,

Holmbridge, Huddersfield,

HD7 1QP.

Tel: 0484 684075.

Gîtes, apartments and mobile-homes.

Clearwater Holidays

17 Heath Terrace,

Leamington Spa, CV32 5NA.

Tel: 0926 450002

Cottages also bareboat yacht charter.

Cosmos

Tourama House, 17 Homesdale Road,

Bromley, BR2 9LX.

Tel: 081 464 3121.

Cottage and motoring holidays.

Country Special Holidays

153b Kidderminster Road, Bewdley, DY12 1JE.

Tel: 0299 403528.

Pottery-making holidays.

Country-wide holidays

Birch Heys, Cromwell Range,

Manchester M14 6HU.

Tel: 061 225 1000.

Walking holidays.

Cresta Holidays

32 Victoria Street,

Altrincham, WA14 1ET.

Tel: 0345 056511.

Group travel, hotels, villas, apartments and holiday villages.

Crystal Holiday Villas

The Courtyard, Arlington Road,

Surbiton, Surrey, KT6 6BW.

Tel: 081 390 3335.

Villa holidays.

Cultural/Educational Services Abroad

44 Sydney Street, Brighton, BN1 4EP.

Tel: 0273 683304.

Language courses.

Cyclists' Touring Club,

69 Meadrow, Godalming,

Surrey, GU7 3HS.

Tel: 04868 7217.

Cycling holidays.

Econocamps

203d, Rumford Shopping Hall, 33 Market Place, Romford, RM1 3AD.

Tel: 0708 21837.

Tent and mobile-home holidays.

En Famille Overseas

The Old Stables, 60b Maltravers St.,
Arundel, BN18 9BG.
Tel: 0903 883266.
Learning French with a French family for teenagers and adults.

Epsom Coaches

Blenheim Road, Epsom, KT19 9AF.
Tel: 03727 27821.
Coach tours.

Euro Academy Outbound

77a George Street, Croydon, CR0 1LD
Tel: 081 686 2363.
Youth travel and language courses.
(Under 26 years).

Eurocamp Independent

Edmundson House, Tatton Street,
Knutsford, Cheshire, WA16 6BG.
Tel: 0565 55399 or 0565 50444.
Campsite booking service.

Eurocamp Travel

Edmundson House, Tatton Street,
Knutsford, WA16 6BG.
Tel: 0565 3844.
Personal callers:
28 Princess Street, Knutsford,
Cheshire.
Tent and mobile-home holidays.

Eurogolf

156 Hatfield Road,
St Albans,
Herts, AL1 4JD.
Tel: 0727 42256.
Golfing holidays.

Europa Mobiles

41–42 High Street, Bideford,

Devon, EX39 3AA.

Tel: 02374 71371.

Mobile-home holidays.

European Canal Cruises

79 Winchester Road, Romsey,

Hants, SO51 8JB.

Tel: 0794 514412.

Hotel barge cruising.

Eurovillas

36 East Street, Coggeshall,

Essex, CO6 1SH.

Tel: 0376 561156.

Villas and farmhouses.

Facet Travel

Oakwood House, Eastern Road,

Wivelsfield Green,

Haywards Heath, RH17 7QH.

Tel: 044484 351.

Art, archaeology and history tours. Châteaux tours/stays.

Coach tours.

Fairway Golfing Holidays

203d Rumford Shopping Hall,

33 Market Place,

Romford, Essex, RM1 3AD.

Tel: 0708 21837.

Golfing holidays.

Farthing Holidays

Holiday House, Weir Road,

Kidworth, LE8 0LQ.

Tel: 0533 796060.

Tailor made lace-makers tours. Coach tours.

France-Directe

2 Church Street,

Warwick. CV34 4AB.

Tel: 0926 497989.

Villa and apartment holidays. Also châteaux tours/stays, health and fitness hotel breaks. Golf holidays.

France Voyages

145 Oxford Street, London W1R 1TB.

Tel: 071 494 3155.

Apartments and studios.

Four Seasons

Springfield, Farsley,

Pudsey, Yorks LS28 5UT.

Tel: 0532 564374.

Mobile-home holidays.

Francophiles Discover France

66 Great Brockeridge,

Westbury-on-Trym, Bristol. BS9 3UA.

Tel: 0272 621975.

Coach, history and gastronomic tours. Also cookery courses.

Freedom in France

Meadows, Poughill,

Bude, Cornwall, EX23 9EN.

Tel: 0288 35591.

Villa and apartment holidays.

French Country Cruises

10 Barley Mow Passage, London W4 4PH.

Tel: 081 995 3642.

Canal cruising.

French Life Motoring Holidays

26 Church Road, Horsforth,

Leeds, LS18 5LG.

Tel: 0532 390077.

Camping, caravanning, *gîte* and motoring holidays. Canal cruising.

The French Selection

Chester Close, Chester Street,

London SW1X 7BQ.

Tel: 071 235 0634.

Châteaux and hotel holidays.

French Travel Service

Georgian House, 69 Boston Manor Road,
Brentford, Middx., TW8 9JQ.
Tel: 081 750 4233.
Hotel, apartment, *gîte* and motoring holidays.

French Villa Centre

175 Selsdon Park Road, Addington,
Croydon, CR2 8JJ.
Tel: 081 651 1231.
Villa, apartment and *gîte* holidays.
Holiday villages.

Gîtes de France

178 Piccadilly, London W1V 9DB.
Tel: 071 493 3480.
Gîtes, hotels and chambres d'hôtes.
Also motoring holidays.

Glenton Tours

114 Peckham Rye, London SE15 4JE.
Tel: 071 639 9777.
Coach tours.

Global Home Exchange and Travel

12 Brookway, London SE3 9BJ.
Tel: 081 852 1439.
Family home exchanges.

Golf en France

Model Farm, Rattlesden, Bury St Edmunds, IP30 0SY.
Tel: 0449 737664.
Golfing holidays.

HF Holidays

142/144 Great North Way,
London NW4 1EG.
Tel: 081 203 0433.
Walking holidays.

Haven Abroad

PO Box 9, Hayling Island, PO11 0NL.

Tel: 0705 466111.

Holidays in luxury caravans.

Home and Overseas Educational Travel

4 Gypsy Hill, London SE19 1NL.

Tel: 081 761 4255.

Group Travel.

Hoseasons Holidays Abroad

Sunway House, Lowestoft,

Suffolk, NR32 3LT.

Tel: 0502 500555.

Gîte and villa holidays. Canal cruising and boat hire.

Hoverspeed Holidays

Maybrook House, Queens Gardens,

Dover. CT17 9UQ.

Tel: 0304 240241.

Villas, cottages, apartments, hotels, and motoring. Holiday village.

ILG Coach and Camping

Devonshire House,

29–31 Elmfield Road,

Bromley BR1 1LT.

Tel: 081 466 6660.

Tent and mobile-home holidays.

Impact Holidays

Devonshire Chambers, 10 Devonshire St,

Carlisle, Cumbria, CA3 8LP.

Tel: 0228 45252.

Camping/caravanning holidays by coach.

I.T.C. Language Schools (Jersey),

Mont les Vaux, St. Aubin, Jersey.

Tel: 0534 41305.

French language courses.

Inn-Active

Inntravel,

The Old Station, Helmsley,

York, YO6 5BZ.

Tel: 0439 71111.

Sailing, cycling and walking holidays.

Insight International Tours

6 Spring Gardens, London SW1A 2BG.

Tel: 071 839 2181.

Coach tours.

Interfrance Reservations

3 Station Parade, London NW2 4NU.

Tel: 081 450 9388.

Hotel reservations service.

Interhome

383 Richmond Road,

Twickenham, TW1 2EF.

Tel: 081 891 1294.

Apartment and cottage holidays.

International Caravan Holidays

9 Wentworth Drive, Lichfield,

Staffs, WS14 9HN.

Tel: 0543 252726.

Caravan and mobile home holidays.

Intervac International Home Exchange

6 Siddals Lane, Allestree,

Derby, DE3 2DY.

Tel: 0332 558931.

Home exchanges.

Just France

1 Belmont, Lansdown Road,

Bath, BA1 5DZ.

Tel: 0225 446328.

Gîtes, villas, apartments. Motoring and hotel holidays.

Keycamp Holidays

92–96 Lind Road

Sutton, Surrey, SM1 4PL.

Tel: 081 661 7334

Camping and mobile-home holidays

Lagrange UK

16–20 New Broadway, London W5 2XA.

Tel: 081 579 7311.

Gîte and apartment holidays.

Motoring/hotel holidays.

L.S.G. in France

201 Main Street, Thornton,

Leics. LE6 1AH.

Tel: 0509 231713 and 0530 230277.

Rambling and nature studies. Courses in French language, painting, photography, regional cookery, arts and crafts.

Leisureline Holidays

Marsh Barn, Ferry Road,

Surlingham, Norwich, NR14 7AR.

Tel: 05088 8193.

Coach holidays.

Erna Low Consultants

9 Reece Mews, London SW7 3HE.

Tel: 071 584 2841.

Health and fitness holidays staying in Thalassotherapy centres/hotels.

Matthews Holidays

8 Bishopsmead Parade,

East Horsley, Surrey, KT24 6RP.

Tel: 04865 4044.

Mobile-home holidays.

Ian Mearns Holidays in France

Priory Lane, Burford,

Oxon. OX8 4SG.

Tel: 099382 2705.

Mobile-home holidays.

Meon Travel

Meon House, Petersfield,

Hants, GU32 3JN.

Tel: 0730 68411.

Villa, apartment and golfing holidays.

National Holidays

George House, George Street,
Wakefield, West Yorks., WF1 1LY.
Tel: 0924 383838 or 387387.
Coach holidays.

David Newman

PO Box 733, 40 Upperton Road,
Eatbourne, Sussex, BN21 4AW.
Tel: 0323 410347.
Gîtes, apartments, hotels, and château hotels.

P&O European Ferries, (Holidays)

Channel House, Channel View Road,
Dover, CT17 9TJ.
Tel: 0304 214422.
Short breaks and motoring holidays.

PLG Adventure Holidays

104 Station Street, Ross on Wye, HR9 7AH.
Tel: 0989 768768.
Young peoples' sailing/windsurfing
holidays with equipment and instruction.

Page and Moy

136–140 London Road,
Leicester, LE2 1EN.
Tel: 0533 552521.
Cookery courses.

Par-Tee Tours

Fairway House, North Road,
Chorley Wood, WD3 5LE.
Tel: 09278 4558..
Group travel, châteaux, golf, tennis, and riding holidays.
Short breaks, cookery courses and thalassotherapy

Phoenix Holidays

16 Bonny Street, London NW1 9PG.
Tel: 071 485 5515.
Villa holidays.

Pleasurewood Holidays

Somerset House, Gordon Road,

Lowestoft, Suffolk, NR32 1PZ.

Tel: 0502 513626.

Gîte and villa holidays.

La Première Villas

Cerbid, Solva, Haverford West,

Pembrokeshire, SA62 6YE.

Tel: 03483 7874.

Villa holidays.

Prime Time Holidays

5a Market Square

Northampton, NN1 2DL.

Tel: 0604 20996

Gîtes and farmhouse B & B.

Les Proprietaires de L'Ouest

Malton House, 24 Hampshire Terrace,

Southsea, Hants, PO1 2QE.

Tel: 0705 755715.

Gîte, villa and apartment holidays.

Quo Vadis

243 Euston Road, London NW1 2BT.

Tel: 071 388 7588.

Villa and apartment holidays.

RAC European Service

PO Box 8, 3–5 Lansdowne Road,

Croydon, CR9 2JH.

Tel: 081 686 2314 or 686 2525.

Hotels, villas, tents, mobile-homes and motoring holidays.

Rendez-vous France

Holiday House, 146–148 London Road,

St Albans, Herts, AL1 1PQ.

Tel: 0727 45400.

Gîte and villa holidays.

Rentavilla

27 High Street, Chesterton,

Cambridge, CB4 1ND.

Tel: 0223 323414.

Villa holidays.

Sally Tours
81 Piccadilly,
London, W1V 9HF.
Tel: 071 355 2266.
Motoring holidays.

SBH France
Cavalier House, Tangmere,
Chichester, West Sussex.
Tel: 0243 773345.
Gîte and villa holidays.

SFV Holidays
Summer House, Hernes Road,
Summertown, Oxford. OX2 7PU.
Tel: 0865 57738.
Gîte, villa, apartment, châteaux and hotel holidays.

Sealink/Dieppe Ferries Holidays
Weymouth Quay, Weymouth, DT4 8DY.
Tel: 0305 777444.
Gîtes, mobile-homes, tents and short-break holidays. Also
holiday villages.

Seasun
71/72 East Hill,
Colchester, CO1 2QW.
Tel: 0206 869888.
Camping and mobile-home holidays.

Select Site Reservations
Travel House, Pandy,
Abergavenny, Gwent, NP7 8DH.
Tel: 0873 890770.
Campsite booking service.

Slipaway Holidays
90 Newland Road, Worthing.
BN11 1LB.
Tel: 0903 214211.

Houses, villas, apartments, canal cruising, motoring and coach tours.

Solaire International Holidays

1158 Stratford Road,

Hall Green,

Birmingham, B28 8AF.

Tel: 021 778 5061.

Tent and mobile-home holidays.

Solgolf Holidays

Centurion House, Bircherley Street,

Hertford, SG14 1BH.

Tel: 0992 501133.

Golfing holidays.

Sparrow Holidays

Fiveacres, Murcott,

Oxford, OX5 2RE.

Tel: 086733 350.

Mobile-home and hotel holidays.

Starvillas

25 High Street, Chesterton,

Cambridge, CB4 1ND.

Tel: 0223 311990.

Villa and apartment holidays.

Martin Sturge

3 Lower Camden Place, Bath, BA1 5JJ.

Tel: 0225 310623.

Holidays in châteaux and *gîtes*.

Sun France

3 Beaufort Gardens, London SW16 3BP.

Tel: 081 679 4562.

Apartment holidays.

Sunselect Villas

60 Crow Hill North,

Middleton, Manchester, M24 1FB.

Tel: 061 655 3055/643 4236.

Gîte, villa and apartment holidays. Canal cruising.

Sunsites
22–24 Princess Street
Knutsford, Cheshire, WA16 6BN.
Tel: 0565 55644.
Tent and mobile-home holidays.

Sunvista Holidays
5a George Street, Warminster,
Wilts, BA12 8QA.
Tel: 0985 217373.
Gîte and villa holidays.

Tourarc UK
197b Brompton Road,
London SW3 1LA.
Tel: 071 589 1918.
Apartment and golfing holidays.

Travelling Together
44 High Street, Meldreth, Herts, SG8 6JU.
Tel: 0763 262190.
Golfing holidays.

Travels with an Interest
165 Gloucester Avenue, London NW1 8LA.
Tel: 071 483 2178.
Sketching holidays.

Triskell Cycle Tours
35 Langland Drive,
Northway, Sedgley, DY3 3TH.
Tel: 09073 78255.
Cycling holidays.

Eric Turrell Travel
Moore House, Moore Road,
Bourton-on-the-Water,
Cheltenham, GL54 2AZ.
Tel: 0451 20927.
Villa holidays.

Ultima Travel
424 Chester Road, Little Sutton,

Wirral, L66 3RB.

Tel: 051 347 1818.

Group travel, youth and school travel.

Unicorn Holidays

Intech House, 33–35 Cam Centre, Wilbury Way,

Hitchin, SG4 0RL.

Tel: 0462 422223.

Holidays in chateaux hotels.

VFB Holidays

Normandy House, Hight Street,

Cheltenham, GL50 3HW.

Tel: 0242 580187.

Cottage and auberge holidays.

VVF

5 Worlds End Lane,

Green Street Green,

Orpington, Kent, BR6 6AA.

Tel: 0689 62904.

Holiday villages.

Vacances en Campagne

Bignor, Pulborough,

West Sussex, RH20 1QD.

Tel: 07987 411.

Self-catering in country houses.

Vacances France

14 Bowthorpe Road, Wisbech,

Cambs, PE13 2DX.

Tel: 0945 587830.

Villa holidays.

Vacations

30–32 Cross Street,

Islington, London N1 2BG.

Tel: 071 359 3511.

Apartment holidays.

Villa France

15 Winchcombe Road, Frampton, Cotterell,

Bristol, BS17 2AG.

Tel: 0454 772410.

Gîte, villa and mobile-home holidays.

Voyages Vacances

4th Floor, 197 Knightsbridge, London SW7 1RB.

Tel: 071 581 5111.

Tennis and golfing holidays.

Wallace Arnold

Gelders Road,

Leeds, LS12 6DH.

Tel: 0532 636456 or 310739.

Coach tours.

Welcome Holidays

18 Kings Drive, Thames Ditton,

K17 0TH.

Tel: 081 398 0355.

Mobile-home holidays.

TOURIST OFFICES and LOISIRS ACCUEIL IN BRITTANY.

For general information on Brittany, towns, resorts, accommodation etc., contact any of the following enclosing an International Reply Coupon.

Regional Tourist Office:

Comité Régional du Tourisme,

3 Rue d'Espagne, BP 4175,

35041 Rennes Cedex.

Tel: 99 50 11 15.

Departmental Offices of Tourism:

Côtes-du-Nord

Comité Départemental du Tourisme,

1 Rue Chateaubriand, BP 620,

22011 St-Brieuc.

Tel: 96 61 66 70.
Finistère
Comité Départemental du Tourisme,
BP 25,
29104 Quimper
Tel: 98 95 28 86.
Ille-et-Vilaine
Comité Départemental du Tourisme,
1 Rue Martenot,
35000 Rennes.
Tel: 99 02 97 43.
Morbihan
Comité Départemental du Tourisme,
BP 400,
56009 Vannes Cedex.
Tel: 97 54 06 56.
In Paris
Maison de la Bretagne
17 Rue de l'Arrivée,
BP 1006, 75737 Paris Cedex.
Tel (1) 45 38 73 15.

Loisirs Accueil

Literally translated is LEISURE WELCOME OFFICE and
is a free booking service set up by most of the Departments.
The English-speaking staff can make reservations for hotels,
gîtes and campsites for individuals and groups. Also many
activity based inclusive holidays and courses.
Loisirs Accueil Côtes-du-Nord
29 Rue des Promenades, BP 620,
22010 St-Brieuc Cedex.
Tel: 96 62 12 40.
Loisirs Accueil Ille-et-Vilaine
1 Rue Martenot,
35000 Rennes.

Tel: 99 02 97 41.

Loisirs Accueil Morbihan

Hôtel du Département,
BP 400, 56009 Vannes Cedex.
Tel: 97 54 06 56.

Tourist Offices in other Countries

French Government Tourist Office, 178 Piccadilly,
London W1V 0AL.
Tel: 071 491 7622.
(Better to write as telephone lines are always busy.)

610 Fifth Avenue,
New York, N.Y. 10020. USA.

9401 Wilshire Boulevard,
Beverly Hills, Los Angeles,
California 90212. USA.

Suite 630
645 North Michigan Ave,
Chicago, Illinois 60611. USA.

World Trade Centre No. 103,
2050 Stemmons Freeway,
Dallas, Texas 75258. USA.

1 Hallidie Plaza, suite 250, San Francisco,
California 94102, USA.

Suite 490, Tour Esso,
1981 Avenue McGill College,
Montreal, Quebec H3A2W9. Canada.

Suite 2405, 1 Dundas Street,
W. Toronto, Ontario M5G1Z3. Canada.

33 Bligh Street, Kindersley House,
Sydney NSW 2000. Australia

Brittany Chamber of Commerce,
8 Creed Lane,
London EC4V 5BR.
Tel: 0860 626596.

YOUTH HOSTELS

To stay at a French Youth Hostel it is necessary to be a
member of the Youth Hostels Association (UK address: 14
Southampton Street, London WC2. Tel: 071 836 1036).

Ligue Francaise pour les Auberges de la Jeunesse,
38 Boulevard Raspail,
75007 Paris.
Tel: (1) 45 48 69 84
run the following:

Camaret-sur-Mer
   Auberge Jeunesse de l'Iroise,
   Route du Toulinguet,
   29570 Camaret-sur-Mer.
   Open 15/6 – 31/9. No station.
   Bus to town centre.
Dinard
   Ker Charles,
   8 Boulevard l'Hôtelier,
   35800 Dinard.
   Tel: 99 46 40 02.
   Open 1/1 – 31/12. 1 km from Dinard Station.
Saint-Lunaire/Dinard
   Les Horizons,
   Rue de Saint-Briac,
   35810 Dinard
   Tel: 99 46 05 05.
   Open 1/1 – 31/12. 3 km from Dinard station.
Lanester

Centre Champêtre de Kerfleau – TY Nevez,
56850 Caudan.
Tel: 97 76 07 68/ 97 81 00 16.
Open 1/1 – 31/12. 5 km from Lorient station.

Pleine-Fougères

Auberge Jeunesse du Mont-St-Michel,
Rue du Normandie,
35610 Pleine-Fougères.
Tel: 99 48 75 69.
Open 1/1 – 31/12. 5 km from Pontorson station.

Saint-Malo

L'Hermitage,
13 Rue des Écoles,
35400 Paramé.
Tel: 99 56 22 00.
Open 1/1 – 31/12. 2 km from St-Malo station.

Trébeurden

Saint-Dominique,
58 Route des Plages,
22560 Trébeurden.
Tel: 96 23 50 05.
Open 1/7 – 31/8. 7 km from Lannion station.

Vannes

New hostel. Details not yet available. Contact – Office du
Tourisme, BP 400, 56009 Vannes.
Tel: 97 54 06 56.

Fédération Unie Des Auberges de Jeunesse,

27 Rue Pajol,
75018 Paris.
Tel: (1) 42 41 59 00.
run the following:

Belle-Ile/Le Palais

Haute Boulogne Belle Ile
56360 Le Palais.
Tel: 97 31 81 33.

Open 1/1 – 31/12. Bus and ferry from Quiberon or Auray.

Belle-Ile-en-Terre

Rue des Ecoles,

22810 Belle-Ile-en-Terre.

Tel: 96 43 30 38. (Mairie)

Open 1/1 – 31/12. 6 km from Belle-Isle-Bégard station and 20 km from Guingamp station.

Concarneau

Place de la Croix,

BP 116, 29900 Concarneau

Tel: 98 97 03 47.

Open 1/1 – 31/12. 13 km from Rosporden station.

Dinan

Moulin de Méen, Vallée de la Fontaine des Eaux,

22100 Dinan.

Tel: 96 39 10 83.

Open 1/1 – 31/12. 2 km from Dinan station.

Fougères

11 Rue Beaumanoir,35300 Fougères.

Tel: 99 99 22 06.

Open 1/1 – 31/12. 1 km from Fougères station.

Ile-de-Batz

Creac'h ar Bolloc'h,

Ecole de Mer,

29253 Ile-de-Batz.

Tel: 98 41 90 41 or 98 61 77 69.

Open 1/4 – 31/10. By boat from Roscoff port.

Ile-de-Groix

Fort du Mene,

56590 Ile-de-Groix.

Tel: 97 05 81 38.

Open 20/3 – 2/10. By ferry from Lorient.

Lannion

6 Rue du 73e Territorial,

22300 Lannion.

Tel; 96 37 91 28.

Open 1/1 – 31/12. Near Lannion station.

Lorient

Rives du Ter,

41 Rue Victor Schoelcher,

56100 Lorient.

Tel: 97 37 11 65.

Open 1/2 – 19/12. 3 km from Lorient station.

Morlaix

3 Route de Paris,

29600 Morlaix.

Tel: 98 88 13 63.

Open 1/1 – 31/12. 2 km from Morlaix station.

Paimpol

Château de Kerraoul,

22500 Paimpol.

Tel: 96 20 83 60.

Open 1/1 – 31/12. 1.5 km from Paimpol.

Pontivy

Ile-des-Recollets

56300 Pontivy.

Tel: 97 25 58 27.

Open 1/1 – 31/12. 1.5 km from Pontivy station.

Quiberon

"Les Filets Bleus",

45 Rue du Roch Priol,

56170 Quiberon.

Tel: 97 50 15 54.

Open 1/1 – 31/12. 1.5 km from Quiberon station.

Quimper

6 Av. des Oiseaux,

Bois de l'Ancien Séminaire,

29000 Quimper.

Tel: 98 55 41 67.

Open 1/1 – 31/12. 2 km from Quimper station.

Rennes

10–12 Canal Saint-Martin,

35700 Rennes.

Tel: 99 33 22 33.

Open 1/1 – 31/12. 3 km from Rennes station.

St-Brieuc

Manoir de la Ville Guyomard,

Les Villages,

22000 St-Brieuc

Tel: 96 78 70 70.

Open 1/1 – 31/12. 3 km from St-Brieuc station.

Saint-Malo

37 Av. du R.P.

Umbricht,

BP 108,

35407 St-Malo Cedex.

Tel: 99 40 29 80.

Open 1/1 – 31/12. 2 km from St-Malo station.

Trébeurden

"Le Toeno",

22560 Trébeurden.

Tel: 96 23 52 22.

Open 1/1 – 31/12. 10 km from Lannion station.